Information Alchemy

Gerald Bernbom, Editor

Information Alchemy

The Art and Science of Knowledge Management

EDUCAUSE
Leadership Strategies No. 3

JOSSEY-BASS
A Wiley Company
San Francisco

This book is part of the Jossey-Bass Higher and Adult Education Series.

Jossey-Bass books and products are available through most bookstores. To contact Jossey-Bass directly, call (888) 378-2537, fax to (800) 605-2665, or visit our website at www.josseybass.com.

Substantial discounts on bulk quantities of Jossey-Bass books are available to corporations, professional associations, and other organizations. For details and discount information, contact the special sales department at Jossey-Bass.

 Manufactured in the United States of America on Lyons Falls Turin Book. This paper is acid-free and 100 percent totally chlorine-free.

Library of Congress Cataloging-in-Publication Data

Information alchemy: the art and science of knowledge management / Gerald Bernbom, editor—1st ed.
    p. cm.—(EDUCAUSE leadership strategies; no. 3) (The Jossey-Bass higher and adult education series)
    Includes bibliographical references and index.
    ISBN 0-7879-5011-4 (pbk.: alk.)
    1. Education, Higher—Information services—Management.   2. Information resources management.   I. Bernbom, Gerald, date.   II. Series.   III. Series: The Jossey-Bass higher and adult education series.
    LB2342.77.154   2000
    378.1'11—dc21   00-010985

FIRST EDITION
PB Printing 10 9 8 7 6 5 4 3 2 1

EDUCAUSE

EDUCAUSE is an international nonprofit association with offices in Boulder, Colorado, and Washington, D.C. The association is dedicated to helping shape and enable transformational change in higher education through the introduction, use, and management of information resources and technologies in teaching, learning, scholarship, research, and institutional management. EDUCAUSE activities include an educational program of conferences, workshops, seminars, and institutes; a variety of print and on-line publications; strategic/policy initiatives such as the National Learning Infrastructure Initiative and the Net@EDU program; a research and development program; and extensive Web-based information services.

EDUCAUSE

- provides professional development opportunities for those involved with planning for, managing, and using information technologies in colleges and universities
- seeks to influence policy by working with leaders in the education, corporate, and government sectors who have a stake in the transformation of higher education through information technologies
- enables the transfer of leading-edge approaches to information technology management and use that are developed and shared through EDUCAUSE policy and strategy initiatives
- provides a forum for dialogue between information resources professionals and campus leaders at all levels
- keeps members informed about information technology innovations, strategies, and practices that may affect their campuses, identifying and researching the most pressing issues

Current EDUCAUSE membership includes more than 1,700 campuses, organizations, and corporations. For up-to-date information about EDUCAUSE programs, initiatives, and services, visit the association's Web site at www.educause.edu, send e-mail to info@educause.edu, or call 303-449-4430.

PRICEWATERHOUSECOOPERS

PricewaterhouseCoopers is a leading provider of professional services to institutions of higher education, serving a full range of educational institutions—from small colleges to large public and private universities to educational companies.

PricewaterhouseCoopers (www.pwcglobal.com) draws on the knowledge and skills of 155,000 people in 150 countries to help clients solve complex business problems and measurably enhance their ability to build value, manage risk, and improve performance.

PricewaterhouseCoopers refers to the U.S. firm of PricewaterhouseCoopers LLP and other members of the worldwide PricewaterhouseCoopers organization.

Contents

List of Tables and Figures

Tables

Figures

Preface

Managing a modern organization depends increasingly on managing the information and knowledge of and about that organization. The information revolution has vastly increased the technical capabilities that are available for storing, analyzing, and transmitting information. New information technology capabilities can add to an organization's effectiveness by improving the ability to gain and use knowledge or to communicate knowledge from one person or place to another. Or the same capabilities can accelerate the loss of knowledge, putting vast amounts of information at risk to destruction or corruption. But as McGee and Prusak (1993, p. 3) note, "Information technology investments create no more value, by themselves, than do investments in new machine tools. . . . The value of information technology depends on information and the role of information in organizations." This book puts the focus of attention on the practices of information and knowledge management in higher education, discussing them in the context of the information technology revolution.

Each chapter addresses an important aspect of knowledge management, identifies key strategic issues of significance to campus leaders, and provides practical advice and guidance to presidents, chancellors, deans, and other leaders on how they might approach these issues. Knowledge management is an interdisciplinary field of study and practice, and the chapter authors represent an array of backgrounds, disciplines, and organizational affiliations.

Knowledge management is fundamentally about the discovery and capture of organizational knowledge, the filtering and arrangement of this knowledge, and the value derived from sharing and using this knowledge throughout the organization. In Chapter One, Jillinda Kidwell, Karen Vander Linde, and Sandra Johnson present a report on the leading edge of professional practice in knowledge management as it is being applied in industry and government, with a focus on the strategic issues and practical implications that are of importance to campus executives. This chapter provides an overview of knowledge management principles, the issues of capturing and using both explicit and tacit knowledge, trends in knowledge management, and knowledge management applications in higher education.

Knowledge management draws on practices and methods by which organizations develop and derive value from their intellectual capital. In Chapter Two, Blaise Cronin and Elisabeth Davenport examine two types of knowledge-based enterprises, drawing comparisons and exploring similarities between higher education and modern consulting organizations. They discuss three approaches to knowledge management: process engineering, by which new knowledge and new value are extracted from existing organizational processes; access engineering, in which value is created through the identification and structuring of an organization's knowledge assets; and cultural engineering, which emphasizes the importance of organizational interaction and learning as prerequisites for the creation and transfer of knowledge.

Thousands of organizations and hundreds of thousands of individuals use networked computing and Internet resources to conduct business and pursue scholarly knowledge. In Chapter Three, Peter Lyman discusses information and network technologies and their impact on knowledge discovery and academic research. He addresses issues of intellectual property and scholarly publishing in a networked world and examines the impact of network technologies on e-commerce practices and their implication for higher education.

Modern organizations, including colleges and universities, increasingly rely on large and complex database systems for the conduct of business and the efficiency of daily operations. These databases can also be analyzed and mined to provide information and knowledge that support strategic decision making. In Chapter Four, Patricia Wallace and Donald Riley explore the technologies of knowledge discovery, beginning with an introduction to information architecture in higher education and proceeding with a discussion of decision support, data warehouses, and on-line analytical processing. This chapter looks ahead to advances in technology for knowledge discovery, including the use of neural networks and expert systems in decision support systems.

Colleges and universities create and manage a variety of records and documents that capture and convey organizational knowledge and that have legal, cultural, or historical significance. Increasingly, these records exist solely in electronic form. In Chapter Five, Anne Gilliland-Swetland addresses key issues about the management and use of organizational records in a digital world, including the requirements for managing records to ensure their authenticity and long-term reliability. She describes the characteristics of organizational records, examines how they function as organizational knowledge assets, and presents the case for why colleges and universities need to pay greater attention to the long-term management and preservation of these potentially fragile digital assets.

Knowledge management has a variety of potential applications in higher education, many of them suggested in the first five chapters of this book. In Chapter Six, Brian Voss presents a case study that describes in detail how knowledge management principles and technologies were applied to information technology support in a university setting. This case study describes and analyzes information technology support as a problem of organizational knowledge management: how to help computer users locate relevant information in a sea of technical documentation, how to put useful information in the hands of computer users when and where they need it, and how to organize the human resources (the know-how) necessary to analyze a computer support problem and find its solution. The Indiana University Knowledge Base and related practices described in this chapter, while designed to address the specific problem of information technology support, may also be viewed as an example of how technology and organization can be applied to knowledge management in other areas.

Chapter Seven summarizes the major recommendations and observations from the preceding six chapters in an action agenda for knowledge management.

Knowledge management can be viewed as a natural successor to information management and, before that, data processing—the next evolutionary step in the transformation of organizations through the ever widening influence of information technology. But knowledge management practices reach beyond the boundaries of computers and networks to include such nontechnical activities as training and development, human resource management, organizational design, intellectual property management, and scholarly communication. Many of these are fundamental to the administration of any modern organization. Some are at the heart of higher education's research and teaching missions. The authors of the chapters that follow provide insights into the principles and practices of knowledge management and their significance to higher education in these early days of the twenty-first century.

Bloomington, Indiana   GERALD BERNBOM
August 2000

Reference

McGee, J., and Prusak, L. *Managing Information Strategically.* New York: Wiley, 1993.

Acknowledgments

I would like to express my sincerest thanks to the authors contributing to this volume, who were so generous in sharing their ideas and insights about knowledge management and who gave freely of their time over the course of months in developing their chapters. Each is a leader in her or his field, and together they represent a rich array of professional backgrounds, academic disciplines, and vital points of view. I feel fortunate as an editor to have had the input and participation of such a distinguished group of scholars and practitioners.

Thanks go as well to EDUCAUSE for its support of this significant series of publications for higher education leaders and for choosing to focus a volume in this series on the important issues of knowledge management.

I would like to thank my colleagues in the Office of the Vice President for Information Technology at Indiana University for their understanding and support as I balanced my editorial responsibilities for this volume with other pressing duties.

Very special thanks go to EDUCAUSE editor Julia Rudy for her generous and helpful assistance in all stages of developing this volume from initial concept through final production. Without her help and direction this volume would not be.

I would also like to thank PricewaterhouseCoopers for their generous support of the EDUCAUSE Leadership Strategies series, which ensures the distribution of each volume to more than 1,700 EDUCAUSE representatives at member campuses, organizations, and corporations.

Finally, my personal thanks go to my wife Charlotte Hess for her unfailing support and encouragement in this endeavor and in so many others.

G.B.

The Authors

Gerald Bernbom is director of research and academic computing and special assistant to the vice president for information technology at Indiana University, with responsibility for digital libraries, massive data storage, and the Indiana University Advanced Visualization Lab. He has been a member of the information technology (IT) organization at Indiana since 1990, with assignments in data administration, video networking, distributed education, and IT strategic planning. In 1997 Bernbom served as a visiting program officer to the Coalition for Networked Information. He has written, presented, and conducted workshops in areas including electronic records management, digital libraries, library-IT partnerships, and institutionwide information strategies.

Blaise Cronin is the James H. Rudy Professor of Information Science and dean of the School of Library and Information Science at Indiana University Bloomington. He is concurrently the Talis Information Visiting Professor of Information Science at the Manchester Metropolitan University in the United Kingdom and a visiting professor of information management at Napier University Business School, Edinburgh, Scotland. Cronin is author or editor of more than two hundred research articles, books, technical reports, and conference papers and was recently appointed editor of the *Annual*

Review of Information Science and Technology. He has taught, conducted research, or consulted in more than thirty countries. Cronin was educated at Trinity College, Dublin, and the Queen's University of Belfast, where he received a Ph.D. and a D.S.Sc.

Elisabeth Davenport is professor of information management at Napier University Business School, Edinburgh, Scotland. She has worked as a member of the faculty at Strathclyde University, Indiana University, and Queen Margaret University College. Davenport has published widely and is a member of several editorial boards, including *The Information Society, Library Quarterly, Annual Review of Information Science and Technology,* and *Journal of Documentation.* Her current areas of research are knowledge management, classification in the workplace, digital genres, interorganizational systems, and social intelligence. She holds degrees in Greek and English literature from Edinburgh University and an M.Sc. and a Ph.D. in information science from Strathclyde University.

Anne J. Gilliland-Swetland is assistant professor in the information studies department of the Graduate School of Education and Information Studies at the University of California at Los Angeles, where she teaches in the graduate specialization in archives and preservation management. She has published widely in the areas of electronic records administration, digital archives, and archival education. Gilliland-Swetland is codirector of the US-InterPARES Project. She holds a Ph.D. from the University of Michigan, an M.S. and a C.A.S. from the University of Illinois at Urbana-Champaign, and an M.A. from Trinity College, Dublin.

Sandra L. Johnson is a director in the education practice of PricewaterhouseCoopers LLP. The education practice coordinates the firm's services to colleges and universities and keeps its higher edu-

cation professionals and clients informed about industry develop-
ments. One of Johnson's responsibilities was to develop Knowledge
Curve, the practice's internal knowledge management database. She
is the author of numerous books and articles on issues affecting
higher education. Johnson holds an M.B.A. from the Simmons College Graduate School of Management and a B.S. from Boston University's School of Public Communications.

Jillinda J. Kidwell is a partner at PricewaterhouseCoopers LLP with
more than eighteen years of experience in the higher education
industry. As a consultant, she has assisted large, research-intensive
universities and their academic medical centers to respond to
external and internal challenges through strategy development,
strategic repositioning, restructuring, and technology implementation. She is the author of numerous books and articles on administrative restructuring in universities and is a frequent speaker on
the subject of transforming higher education through process
redesign, organizational restructuring, and change management.
Kidwell holds an M.B.A. from Tulane University and a B.A. from
Calvin College.

Peter Lyman is professor and associate dean in the School of Information Management and Systems at the University of California,
Berkeley. He is completing an ethnography of a Silicon Valley
dot-com start-up company that is focused on the higher education
market. The courses he teaches are in the areas of information
management skills and the management of organizational change
and innovation made possible by information technologies. Current papers and course syllabi are available on his Web site at
www.sims.berkeley.edu/~plyman. Lyman holds a B.A. in philoso-
phy from Stanford University, an M.A. in political science from
the University of California, Berkeley, and a Ph.D. in political science from Stanford University.

Donald R. Riley is associate vice president and chief information officer (CIO) at the University of Maryland, College Park, and a professor in the Decision Information Technologies division of the Robert H. Smith School of Business. Previously he was CIO at the University of Minnesota and was on the faculty of the mechanical engineering department there for more than twenty years. His research and teaching interests include interactive computer graphics, knowledge-based systems for design and manufacturing, and computer-aided design. He has published over one hundred refereed technical papers and several copyrighted software packages for computer-aided design. Riley received his B.S.M.E., M.S.M.E., and Ph.D. degrees from Purdue University.

Karen M. Vander Linde is a partner with PricewaterhouseCoopers (PwC) and a senior partner in PwC's Center for Performance Improvement, specializing in technology assimilation, learning, and knowledge management solutions. She is a leader of the PwC knowledge management practice for the Americas and an active member of PwC's global knowledge management team. In this capacity, she helps develop leading-edge knowledge management systems for clients and for PwC's internal operations and leads PwC's knowledge management study with the Conference Board. Vander Linde holds a B.A. in English and history from Kalamazoo College, an M.A. in English and communications from the University of Illinois, and has all but completed her dissertation for an Ed.D. in human resources development and business management from George Washington University.

Brian D. Voss is associate vice president for telecommunications at Indiana University, responsible for the university's telecommunications organization, including voice, data, and video networks. He has over sixteen years of leadership experience across the information technology field in both higher education and the private sector, spanning operations and production services, application development, user support, and telecommunications. Voss is the architect of the university's leveraged support model and was a key player in developing institutional software licensing agreements, including the groundbreaking agreement with Microsoft negotiated by Indiana University in 1998. He has been a leader in the initiative to provide life-cycle funding for IT infrastructure throughout the university.

Patricia M. Wallace is executive director of the Center for Knowledge and Information Management and acting director of the Netcentricity Program at the Robert H. Smith School of Business, University of Maryland, College Park. Her career as a faculty member, researcher, consultant, and chief information officer has spanned the fields of technology and human behavior. She is author of several books, software programs, and many articles covering technology strategy, knowledge management, distance education, and related subjects. Her most recent book, *The Psychology of the Internet*, deals with the Internet's effects on human behavior; it is currently being translated into five languages. She holds a Ph.D. in psychology from the University of Texas at Austin and an M.S. in computer systems management from the University of Maryland University College.

Information Alchemy

Applying Corporate Knowledge Management Practices in Higher Education

Jillinda J. Kidwell, Karen M. Vander Linde, Sandra L. Johnson

Once upon a time, there was a top-rated restaurant that specialized in fine dining, featuring regional cuisine and locally grown produce. The restaurant—which we will call Foster's—proved to be such a successful financial venture that the owner-chef decided to semiretire at a young age. He sold his restaurant to a national restaurant conglomerate but stayed on to experiment and plan innovative menus.

Foster's joined two other fine dining restaurants in the conglomerate's portfolio, which also included three ethnic and three theme restaurants. All nine restaurants reported to a director of restaurant operations, who reported to the senior management team. A finance, human resource, and sales-marketing unit supported the restaurant operations.

Despite the differences in their cuisine and geographic locations, the nine restaurants had much in common, and all stood to gain by

We appreciate the contributions to this chapter of several PricewaterhouseCoopers colleagues: Deborah Furey and Dorothy Yu for Figure 1.1, Michael Sousa for Tables 1.2 through 1.6, and Richard Warrick for the section on new trends in knowledge management.

sharing their collective knowledge about five basic activities on which
they all depended:

- Using recipes

- Buying ingredients (and perhaps saving money by buying in bulk)

- Operating kitchens and dining rooms, hiring and training chefs
  and waiters centrally

- Honing cooking techniques (especially learning from one another)

- Innovating by developing new recipes

The owner-chef of Foster's, who excelled at innovation, had original ideas for each of the other restaurants and developed new
recipes for them. And when one of the ethnic restaurants received
excellent reviews for prompt, friendly service, senior managers visiting
the other restaurants were able to share this restaurant's best practices, enabling all of them to improve customer service.

The moral of the story? There is great value for organizations that
are willing to share knowledge. And sharing knowledge is a fundamental tenet of knowledge management.

Are the concepts of knowledge management applicable to colleges and universities? Some would argue that sharing knowledge is
their raison d'être. If that is the case, then the higher education sector should be replete with examples of institutions that leverage
knowledge to spur innovation, improve customer service, or achieve
operational excellence. However, although some examples exist,
they are the exception rather than the rule. Knowledge management is a new field, and experiments are just beginning in higher
education.

We believe there is tremendous value to higher education institutions that develop initiatives to share knowledge to achieve
business objectives. This chapter outlines the basic concepts of
knowledge management as it is applied in the corporate sector, considers trends, and explores how it might be applied in higher education.

Knowledge Basics

Knowledge management is the process of transforming information and intellectual assets into enduring value. It connects people with the knowledge that they need to take action, when they need it. In the corporate sector, managing knowledge is considered key to achieving breakthrough competitive advantage.

Knowledge starts as data, raw facts, and numbers—for example, the market value of an institution's endowment. Information is data put into context—in the same example, the endowment per student at a particular institution. Information is readily captured in documents or in databases; even large amounts are fairly easy to retrieve with modern information technology systems.

Before acting on information, however, we need to take one more step. Only when information is combined with experience and judgment does it become knowledge. Knowledge can be highly subjective and hard to codify. It includes the insight and wisdom of employees. It may be shared through e-mailed "best practices" memos or even sticky notes on a cubicle wall. And once we have knowledge, we can put it to work and apply it to decision making.

A popular framework for thinking about knowledge (Koulopoulos and Frappaolo, 1999; Polanyi, 1967) proposes two main types of knowledge: explicit and tacit (see Figure 1.1). Explicit knowledge is documented information that can facilitate action. It can be expressed in formal, shared language. Examples include formulas, equations, rules, and best practices. Explicit knowledge is:

- Packaged

- Easily codified

- Communicable

- Transferable

Tacit knowledge is know-how and learning embedded within the minds of the people in an organization. It involves perceptions, insights, experiences, and craftsmanship. Tacit knowledge is:

- Personal

- Context specific

- Difficult to formalize

- Difficult to communicate

- More difficult to transfer

Most business actions require the guidance of both explicit and tacit knowledge.

In organizations, knowledge originates in individuals, but it is embodied in teams and organizations, as shown in Figure 1.1. In an organization, examples of explicit knowledge are strategies, methodologies, processes, patents, products, and services. Examples of tacit knowledge in an organizational context are skills and competencies, experiences, relationships within and outside the organization, individual beliefs and values, and ideas.

Knowledge also is embedded in work processes, and it exists in all core functions of an organization as well as in its systems and infrastructure. Effective knowledge management programs identify and leverage the know-how embedded in work, with a focus on how it will be applied. The challenge in knowledge management is to make the right knowledge available to the right people at the right time.

The Importance of Knowledge Management in the Corporate Sector

Many corporations believe that knowledge management is increasingly important to competitive success because it helps achieve business results in three core areas: innovation, customer intimacy, and operational excellence.

PricewaterhouseCoopers conducted a survey in 1999 of chief executives from nineteen countries. Among the survey respondents, 97

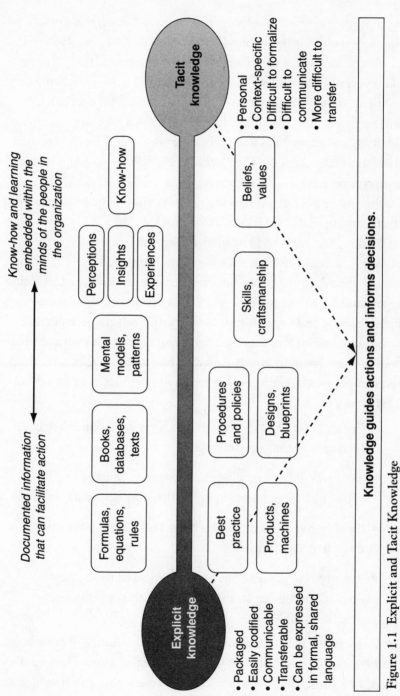

Documented information that can facilitate action

Know-how and learning embedded within the minds of the people in the organization

Tacit knowledge

- Personal
- Context-specific
- Difficult to formalize
- Difficult to communicate
- More difficult to transfer

Beliefs, values

Know-how

Perceptions

Insights

Experiences

Skills, craftsmanship

Mental models, patterns

Procedures and policies

Designs, blueprints

Books, databases, texts

Best practice

Products, machines

Formulas, equations, rules

Explicit knowledge

- Packaged
- Easily codified
- Communicable
- Transferable
- Can be expressed in formal, shared language

Knowledge guides actions and informs decisions.

Figure 1.1 Explicit and Tacit Knowledge

Source: Copyright 2000 PricewaterhouseCoopers LLP.

percent identified knowledge management as "absolutely critical" to the success of their companies (PricewaterhouseCoopers, 1999, p. 3).

According to Louis V. Gerstner, Jr., chairman of IBM, "The age-old levers of competition—labor, capital, and land—are being supplemented by knowledge, and the most successful companies . . . will be those that . . . exploit knowledge about customer behavior, markets, and economies and technology faster and more effectively than their competitors. They will use knowledge to adapt quickly, seizing opportunities and improving products and services, of course, but just as important, renewing the way they define themselves, think, and operate" (Hackett, 2000, p. 4).

Linking learning and knowledge management can be extremely powerful. PricewaterhouseCoopers also sponsored the 1999 Conference Board survey of two hundred senior executives at 158 global companies. The survey describes the current state of knowledge management and organizational learning from the perspective of senior line and staff executives. Participating organizations, 85 percent of them based in North America, had an average of forty thousand employees, and 68 percent reported revenues over $5 million. The survey found that:

- Eighty percent of the companies have some knowledge management efforts under way.

- Six percent use knowledge management enterprisewide; 60 percent expect to do so in five years.

- Twenty-five percent have a chief knowledge officer or chief learning officer.

- Twenty-one percent have communicated their knowledge management strategy widely in the organization (Hackett, 2000).

Corporate CEOs' comments about the importance of knowledge could apply to universities as well. The most successful universities should be those that use knowledge to renew the way they define themselves, think, and operate.

The Value Proposition

Once the organization recognizes the importance of knowledge management, the next step is to use it strategically. In our work with corporate clients, we advocate applying knowledge management to three fundamental value propositions: innovation, customer intimacy, and operational excellence. Each of these drivers is explored in Table 1.1, and each is illustrated with one or more case studies in the sections that follow.

Innovation

Warner-Lambert, the giant pharmaceutical and health care products provider that is merging with Pfizer, illustrates using knowledge management to enhance innovation. One of the company's

Table 1.1. Aligning Business Goals with Knowledge Strategies

Driver	Defining the Business Goal	Best Knowledge Strategy
Innovation	To become more competitive by consistently providing more innovative products or services	To leverage internal and external knowledge and relationships to build more innovative products or services or build knowledge products or services for profit
Customer intimacy	To establish profitable, loyal relationships to enhance the long-term economic value of customers	To leverage customer knowledge and relationships to build better services and products
Operational excellence	To achieve efficient and effective operations through high-quality, consistent processes	To identify, create, and leverage process knowledge to enhance performance and process design

products is Lipitor, a market-leading cholesterol-reducing agent. To increase the speed of getting this product to market, Warner-Lambert used knowledge management to transform the product launch. The company created a CD-ROM to provide all the clinical, regulatory, and marketing information necessary to launch the product. Distributed worldwide, it facilitated a homogeneous launch in approximately sixty countries, increasing the speed of approvals country to country. In the future, product launches will use the Internet instead of a CD-ROM, but most packages will still be built around a specific process, whether it is going to market, completing an alliance, or transferring best practices.

As in the corporate sector, using knowledge innovatively can help state governments achieve challenging goals. For example, the state of California cannot train as many teachers on its campuses as it needs over the next few years. The numbers are staggering; California estimates it will need as many as 250,000 new teachers over the next decade as its public K–12 school population increases by 150,000 students annually (California State University Institute for Education Reform, 1998). Traditional approaches to recruiting students to the field of teaching will not produce enough teachers to meet the demand.

In 1997, Governor Pete Wilson and the California legislature established an innovative program, the California Center for Teaching Careers (CalTeach), to recruit qualified people into teaching. The CalTeach World Wide Web site (www.calteach.com) is an information and referral recruitment center for individuals who are considering a career in education. The site helps to match school districts that want to recruit new teachers with those who are seeking teaching jobs. It also contains information about teacher recruitment programs based in high schools and colleges throughout the state. This site has attracted over 6 million hits since it went live on May 5, 1998. The Internet and intranets are common vehicles for knowledge management.

Customer Intimacy

Sequent Computer Systems is a small company that competes at the high end of the UNIX systems market against such industry giants as IBM and Sun Microsystems. To remain competitive against firms with substantial resources, a small company like Sequent must find a way to level the playing field. Sequent used knowledge management to give its direct sales force a leg up on the competition.

Sequent's knowledge management tool is the Sequent Corporate Electronic Library (SCEL). Through an intranet application, SCEL captures best practices, proposals, and frequently asked questions (FAQs). In short, it provides one-stop shopping for the design, sales, and marketing teams. The site also is integrated with the firm's on-line price book, a customer database, and the corporate telephone directory. According to Sequent's knowledge management leaders, SCEL has helped the organization increase average selling price and reduce delivery and response time in the sales and post-sales process (O'Dell and Grayson, 1998).

The goal of enhancing customer intimacy is likely to resonate with those in the higher education sector. For example, one large public university that was perceived as being unfriendly to students needed a mechanism to change its image—and fast. In an effort to attract and retain more students, the university used its Web site to integrate student services and put the students more in control. It established a student services portal as a place where students could access, at any time from any place, a powerful database to guide them through the maze of multiple offices and systems. From one site, students can now perform transactions from registering for classes, to viewing their grades, to finding which courses get good student reviews.

The university plans to take the customer experience to the next level and integrate services in a way that matches how the student wants to view them. Importantly, students can perform what-if scenarios and explore what happens if they change majors. Will it take longer to graduate? Will financial aid increase or decrease?

As each college generation moves on, it will become increasingly important for higher education to focus on building a strong on-line intimacy. Students will expect it, and it will form the basis of an increasingly important relationship with their alma mater. Just as experiences with good teachers, counselors, and friendly financial aid officers often influence how involved alumni will be in the institution after graduation, the quality of the Web portal can be used as a tool to tie alumni back to a school after graduation. After years of using their university's portal, graduates will view it as an old and familiar friend.

Operational Excellence

The former commander in chief of the U.S. Navy's Pacific Fleet, Admiral Archie Clemins, commanded the world's largest fleet— almost 200 ships, 1,400 aircraft, and 220,000 military and civilian personnel. Integrating such a vast fleet so that each part knows what the other is doing is challenging but absolutely essential. For this reason, Clemins was a firm supporter of IT-21, an ambitious initiative to construct a high-speed computer network—effectively an intranet—to link the ships of the Pacific Fleet with their command centers on shore, as well as their satellites, aircraft, and the Pentagon. When this multimillion-dollar investment in hardware and software is completed in 2001, the fleet will be fully linked and able to maneuver its resources fast and cohesively.

Recognizing that it must change its processes to leverage this technology fully, the Navy launched a program called the Solution Provider Initiative. Its objective is to design and implement knowledge management, communications, and enterprise resource planning programs that take maximum advantage of the new technology. The Solution Provider Initiative is putting the Navy squarely on the leading edge of reengineering in the government sector.

Commander Nancy Jenkins, the fleet's knowledge manager, demonstrates the capabilities of IT-21 when, with a few clicks of the mouse, her screen is filled with the Knowledge Homeport, the front page of the intranet site. The Knowledge Homeport serves as the access point to a wealth of information for the Navy staff members. It also serves as a portal to the external information and technology forums within the Navy, linking naval commands located around the globe. Important updates on various aspects of staff activities scroll across a marquee on the home page. This site is one of the first outcomes of the Solution Provider Initiative.

Examples of operational excellence also exist in higher education. According to a news item in the March 29, 2000, issue of *Edupage* (EDUCAUSE, 2000), Pennsylvania State University, Ohio University, and Washington State University have realized substantial efficiencies since implementing Web-based document management and knowledge management systems. At Penn State, the accounting, human resource, administration, and physical plant offices adopted knowledge management and document management systems. On average, 80 percent of job applicants now submit their applications and résumés electronically to the human resource office. The remaining paper and fax applications are imported or scanned into the system. As a result of the new system, Penn State interviews applicants and fills positions much faster than before. The institution also has reduced the number of employees handling the applications.

Washington State University's admissions department is implementing a document management system to handle the ten thousand undergraduate admission applications it receives every year. The university is using a system that includes scanning, queuing, and workflow technologies, enabling it to simplify and reduce the amount of paperwork in the application process. In a similar move, Ohio University is transferring its 140,000 legacy documents to Web-based storage and access systems.

New Trends in Knowledge Management

Several trends will shape the field of knowledge management in the not-too-distant future:

- Emerging technology solutions

- The convergence of knowledge management with e-business

- The movement from limited knowledge management projects to more enterprisewide projects

- Increasing use of knowledge management to enhance innovation

- Increasing use of tacit knowledge (rather than explicit knowledge)

Emerging Technology Solutions

Lotus Notes, the software that packaged e-mail with data repositories and basic collaborative tools, was the first catalyst for knowledge management. Since Notes, most knowledge management applications (including later versions of Notes) have migrated to intranet-friendly, Web-based platforms. Currently available solutions for search and retrieval, e-mail, collaboration, and so forth are much better today than they were even a year ago. However, no single application does all of these things well.

It is likely that the next "killer application" for knowledge management will be the corporate portal—a gateway to applications that integrate collaborative tools, business intelligence, and unstructured text search capabilities. Portals started as a way to organize a variety of Web-based information sources on one desktop interface: a search tool, news feeds, links to favorite Web sites, content organized by topic, and so forth. Corporate portals do the same thing, allowing users to customize their desktops to show information from a variety of sources within the organization (and usually from outside the firewall as well).

Some universities are already making use of the corporate portal concept. For example, one major state university system is developing Web-based portals to deliver integrated services previously addressed in a very disaggregated fashion. The business objectives of the first portal—for the university's central administration—include institutional marketing, creating brand identity, building community with prospective students and parents, becoming the gateway for finding information about university resources and programs, and providing a rich information environment for decision making. The portal serves multiple functions for multiple customers with one tool.

Development of a second, similar portal supports the vision of a new intercampus collaborative for teaching and learning with technology. That vision calls for uniting the collective interests and goals of the campuses in the system in nurturing excellence in the use of technology for teaching and learning. The portal will improve the efficiency of knowledge exchange and deliver a set of shared business objectives that include communications around best practices, a gateway to research on the use of teaching and learning through technology, professional development, policy development and review, and resource development. The portal provides faculty members at the individual campuses with efficient, direct links to current knowledge about teaching and learning through technology among the campuses of the university system, nationally, and internationally.

Convergence with E-Business

The trend toward portals as the technology tool of choice for knowledge leads to another trend: the convergence of knowledge management and e-business. One reason for this trend is that the Web-based technologies that support e-business are now being applied to support knowledge management (and vice versa). A more powerful reason is that both disciplines are about creating conversations, sharing knowledge, and building communities. Knowledge management has been about breaking down barriers within the organization, and e-business has been about breaking down barriers between the organization and its customers.

A major application of the convergence of e-business and knowledge management will be in managing business-to-business customer relationships. Extending the organization's communities to include the customer in the generation and exchange of knowledge promises to be an effective competitive advantage.

From Limited Projects to Holistic Programs

As knowledge management matures as a corporate discipline, more companies will gravitate toward a more holistic approach to it. Research shows that although many companies have begun to develop some sort of knowledge management capability, very few (6 percent) have implemented knowledge management programs on an enterprisewide scale. Over the past two or three years, a company could be recognized as a best-practices exemplar of knowledge management by having a single successful initiative—for having developed a robust intranet, for instance, or initiating communities of practice or redesigning a core business process around knowledge sharing.

This early tendency to focus on one type of initiative has fueled the debate between experts advocating a technocentric approach to knowledge management and those advocating a learning-centric approach. Organizations are already realizing that it does no good to have robust technology solutions if the existing culture prevents knowledge sharing and, conversely, that it does little good to have pockets of robust knowledge sharing without some technological means of making knowledge widely accessible.

As organizations share their lessons learned about implementing knowledge management programs, some are discovering the interdependent nature of knowledge management capabilities. They are finding that a balanced portfolio of knowledge management initiatives yields the best results and that excelling at technology-related capabilities does not preclude excelling at people- or process-related capabilities. (In fact, excelling in one area may well depend on excelling in another.)

Moving from Best Practices to Innovation

The Conference Board survey report cited earlier indicated that most knowledge management programs are still focused on creating repositories for storing and diffusing best practices, focusing on operational excellence and cost reduction (Hackett, 2000). While many companies have earned a significant payback from these efforts, the real payoff may lie in applying knowledge management to spur innovation.

Nokia is a good example of a company that has applied knowledge management to encourage innovation in its R&D and product development functions. The company uses knowledge management practices to make sense of market trends and customer requirements and quickly puts that knowledge to action in the product development pipeline. Industry analysts report that Nokia delivers a new mobile communication product about every twenty-five days.

Advances in Working with Tacit Knowledge

Explicit knowledge, which consists of formulas, equations, rules, and best practices, is easier to work with than tacit knowledge, which involves perceptions, experiences, and insights, because it can be recorded, stored in databases, and transported easily. The problem is that it is a little too portable—if you have it today, your competitors will likely have it tomorrow. And in any case, the mechanics of managing explicit knowledge are sufficiently well known that it will not provide a lasting competitive advantage.

The ability to manage tacit knowledge, on the other hand, promises to deliver huge returns for organizations that learn to use it effectively. The reason is that in the most valuable knowledge-intensive businesses—software development, say, or product design—the difference between a good performer and the best performer is huge. And the difference that matters most lies in tacit knowledge: a deep understanding of how to act on knowledge effectively.

Applying Knowledge Management in Higher Education

Using knowledge management techniques and technologies in higher education is as vital as it is in the corporate sector. If done effectively, it can lead to better decision-making capabilities, reduced "product" development cycle time (for example, curriculum development and research), improved academic and administrative services, and reduced costs.

Consider the number of faculty and staff who possess institutional knowledge. For example, what institution does not have a faculty member who has led successful curriculum revision task forces? Or a departmental secretary who knows how to navigate the complex proposal development or procurement processes? Or a researcher who has informal connections to the National Science Foundation? Or a special assistant to the president who has uncovered (or generated) useful reports that individual deans or department chairs could use to develop their own strategic plans?

Relying on the institutional knowledge of unique individuals can hamper the flexibility and responsiveness of any organization. The challenge is to convert the information that currently resides in those individuals and make it widely and easily available to any faculty member, staff person, or other constituent.

An institutionwide approach to knowledge management can lead to exponential improvements in sharing knowledge—both explicit and tacit—and the subsequent surge benefits. Tables 1.2 through 1.6 illustrate how knowledge management applications

Table 1.2. Application and Benefits of Knowledge Management for the Research Process

Knowledge Management Application	Benefits
A repository of: • Research interests within an institution or at affiliated institutions (potential subcontractors) • Research results (where possible) and funding organizations (federal agencies, foundations, and corporations) with easy search capabilities to facilitate interdisciplinary opportunities • Commercial opportunities for research results A portal for research administration procedures and best practices related to: • Funding opportunities • Prepopulated proposals, budgets, and protocols • Proposal routing policies and procedures • Award notification, account setup, and negotiation policies and procedures • Contract and grant management policies and procedures • Technical and financial report templates and policies and procedures • Overview of internal services, resources, and staff	• Increased competitiveness and responsiveness for research grants, contracts, and commercial opportunities • Reduced turnaround time for research • Minimized devotion of research resources to administrative tasks • Facilitation of interdisciplinary research • Leveraging of previous research and proposal efforts • Improved internal and external services and effectiveness • Reduced administrative costs

Table 1.3. Application and Benefits of Knowledge Management for the Curriculum Development Process

Knowledge Management Application	Benefits
• Repository of curriculum revision efforts that includes research conducted, effectiveness measures, best practices, and lessons learned • Repository of content modularized and arranged to facilitate interdisciplinary curriculum design and development • Portal of information related to teaching and learning with technology, including faculty development opportunities, outcomes tracking, lessons learned, best practices, and technology overviews • Hubs of information in each disciplinary area, including updated materials, recent publications, and applicable research • Repository of pedagogy and assessment techniques, including best practices, outcomes tracking, faculty development opportunities, and research • Repository of analyzed student evaluations updated each semester for lessons learned and best practices for all faculty	• Enhanced quality of curriculum and programs through identifying and leveraging best practices and monitoring outcomes • Improved speed of curriculum revision and updating • Enhanced faculty development efforts, especially for new faculty • Improved administrative services related to teaching and learning with technology • Improved responsiveness through monitoring and incorporating lessons learned from the experiences of colleagues, student evaluations, and corporate or other constituent input

Table 1.3. Application and Benefits of Knowledge Management for the Curriculum Development Process (*continued*)

Knowledge Management Application	Benefits
• Portal for new faculty with guides for developing curriculum, working with senior faculty, establishing effective teaching styles, advising do's and don'ts, supervising Ph.D. students, and so forth	• Interdisciplinary curriculum design and development facilitated by navigating across departmental boundaries
• Repository of corporate relationships to identify curriculum design advisory task forces, guest speakers, adjuncts, case study sites, and so forth	

could benefit a number of university processes and services: the research process, curriculum development process, student and alumni services, administrative services, and strategic planning.

Is Higher Education Ready to Embrace Knowledge Management?

A key ingredient in an institution's readiness to embrace knowledge management is its culture—the beliefs, values, norms, and behaviors that are unique to an organization. Informally, it is the unwritten rules, or "how things really get done" (Hackett, 2000).

Table 1.7 shows the cultural shift that occurs in everyday language from a traditional environment to one in which sharing knowledge has become ingrained. Higher education is moving from the old culture that considers, "What's in it for me?" to a new culture that says, "What's in it for our customer?" And it is developing a culture that is ready to embrace knowledge management.

Table 1.4. Application and Benefits of Knowledge Management for Student and Alumni Services

Knowledge Management Application	Benefits
• Portal for student services for both students and faculty and staff at the institution so that they are well informed to advise students. Information could include policies and procedures related to admissions, financial aid, registration, degree audit, billing, payment process, advising and tutoring, housing, dining, and other services. This portal could be personalized for individual schools or student groups to customize service offerings. • Portal for career placement services (potentially part of a large portal for all corporate connections) to provide a one-stop service center for students, and also for faculty and staff in order to ensure they are informed. • Repository of student affairs services for faculty and staff to ensure that all constituents understand existing services and can provide proper advising. • Portal for alumni and development services to minimize redundant efforts, capture contact reports, and link to research, curriculum, and career development efforts. • Portal for information on outreach constituents to integrate efforts and minimize redundant efforts.	• Improved services for students • Improved service capability of faculty and staff • Improved services for alumni and other external constituents • Improved effectiveness and efficiency of advising efforts (to integrate fragmented efforts currently undertaken by faculty, academic support staff, student services staff, and student affairs staff)

Table 1.5. Application and Benefits of Knowledge Management for Administrative Services

Knowledge Management Application	Benefits
• Portal for financial services (that is, budgeting and accounting) that includes FAQs, best practices, procedures, templates, and communities of interest to share information and serve as an impetus for improvement efforts • Portal for procurement (that is, purchasing, accounts payable, receiving, warehousing) that includes FAQs, best practices, procedures, templates, and communities of interest (for example, by commodity, purchasing vehicle, or vendor) to share information and serve as an impetus for improvement efforts (for example, leverage lessons learned from others in the institution or design on-line vendor sites such as Web-based catalogues) • Portal for human resources (that is, vacancy to hire, payroll, affirmative action, and so forth) that includes FAQs, best practices, procedures, templates, and communities of interest to share information and serve as an impetus for improvement efforts	• Improved effectiveness and efficiency of administrative services • Enhanced ability to identify improvement efforts • Improved ability to support the trend toward decentralization (for example, local business centers), by providing guidelines for consistency • Improved compliance with administrative policies such as procurement preferred vendors, procurement card policies, budgeting procedures, and affirmative action guidelines • Improved responsiveness and communication capabilities

Table 1.6. Application and Benefits of Knowledge Management for Strategic Planning

Knowledge Management Application	Benefits
• Office of Knowledge Management, emerging from the previous Office of Institutional Research • Portal for internal information that catalogues the strategic plans, reports developed for external audiences (for example, IPEDS, accreditation reports, others), clear data definitions, presentations by executives, and so forth • Portal for external information, including benchmark studies, environmental scans, competitor data, links to research groups, higher education research groups and publications, and presentations by executives • Monthly market watch developed in tandem with admissions, continuing education, alumni and development, and others that documents key trends and potential implications • Repository of data related to accountability and outcomes tracking by monitoring assessments, performance indicators, benchmarking, and so forth	• Improved ability to support the trend toward decentralized strategic planning and decision making (for example, block budgeting, responsibility center management). Better information leads to better decisions. • Improved sharing of internal and external information minimizes redundant efforts and lessens the reporting burden plaguing many institutions today. • Better ability to develop up-to-date and market-focused strategic plans. • Shared knowledge from a variety of constituents to begin to create a learning organization that is responsive to market trends.

Table 1.7. The Changing Vocabulary

Old Culture	New Culture
"What's in it for me?"	"What's in it for our customer?"
Task forces selected by management	Knowledge-sharing communities
"It's not my job."	"How can we help?"
Inward—top management focus	Outward—customer focus
Functional silos	Cross-functional teams
Knowledge hoarding is power	Knowledge sharing is valued
Culture of blame	Culture of accountability
Information available on a need-to-know basis	Open-book philosophy
Focus on key employees and experts	Focus on entire workforce—learn from each other

Source: Hackett (2000). Copyright 2000 The Conference Board.

As institutions launch knowledge management initiatives, they can learn lessons from their counterparts in the corporate sector:

- Start with strategy. Before doing anything else, determine what you want to accomplish with knowledge management.

- Organizational infrastructure—human resources, financial measurements of success, and information technology—should support knowledge management. Think of technology as an enabler, and measure the impact of knowledge management in financial terms, such as cost reductions, customer satisfaction, and speed to market.

- Seek a high-level champion for the initiative—someone who believes in its benefits and can advocate as needed.

- Select a pilot project for knowledge management—ideally one with high impact on the organization but of low risk—to build credibility for knowledge management. If possible, make the pilot one that participants will enjoy and find rewarding.

- Develop a detailed action plan for the pilot that defines the process, the information technology infrastructure, and the roles and incentives of the pilot project team.

- After the pilot, assess the results and refine the action plan.

Conclusion

Colleges and universities have significant opportunities to apply knowledge management practices to support every part of their mission—from education to public service to research. Knowledge management should not strike higher education institutions as a radically new idea; rather, it is a new spin on their raison d'être. But implementing knowledge management practices wisely is a lesson that the smartest organizations in the corporate and not-for-profit sectors are learning all over again.

References

California State University Institute for Education Reform. "CalTeach." [www.csus.edu/ier/calteach.html]. 1998.

EDUCAUSE. "Edupage." [www.educause.edu/pub/edupage/edupage.html]. Mar. 29, 2000.

Hackett, B. *Beyond Knowledge Management: New Ways to Work.* New York: The Conference Board, 2000.

Koulopoulos, T. M., and Frappaolo, C. *Smart Things to Know About Knowledge Management.* Dover, N.H.: Capstone US, 1999.

O'Dell, C., and Grayson, C. J., Jr., with Essaides, N. *If Only We Knew What We Know.* New York: Free Press, 1998.

Polanyi, M. *The Tacit Dimension.* New York: Routledge, 1967.

PricewaterhouseCoopers. *Intersections,* Feb.–Mar. 1999, p. 1.

2

Knowledge Management in Higher Education

Blaise Cronin, Elisabeth Davenport

Knowledge management is a key competence in organizations that nurture and harvest intellectual capital. In this chapter, we examine two examples of such knowledge-intensive organizations: the for-profit consulting firm and the not-for-profit university. As the boundaries between the two types of organizations begin to blur, the consulting firm provides a useful model for university administrators who are interested in applying knowledge management principles and techniques.

Major consulting firms have been enthusiastic and early adopters of knowledge management (Sarvary, 1999). Their ability to generate and retain business is a function of their proprietary expertise, collective know-how, cumulative industry experience, and capacity for original thinking. Their principal assets are intangible and, in the case of their human intellectual capital base, often scattered and highly mobile.

One key challenge that knowledge-intensive professional practices face is converting human intellectual capital into structural intellectual capital, or institutionalizing and formalizing that which is often localized, individualized, and embedded in practice (Stewart, 1997). Authorities estimate that McKinsey and Company, an international consulting firm, spends between $50 million and $100 million a year on "knowledge building" (Crainer and Dearlove, 1999, p. 63), and KPMG Consulting is committed to investing approximately 1 percent of its $10 billion in revenues in knowledge management. The motivations behind such investments are both defensive and offensive. By investing in knowledge management, firms minimize the effects of theft and inadvertent leakage or loss as a consequence of staff departures or defections. Further, they build a smarter organization by letting the whole company learn from best practices and by tapping institutional memory (Stein, 1995). Building social network connectivity is a critical aspect of managing a dispersed, knowledge-based professional practice, but it poses a major challenge.

Universities are knowledge-intensive and reflexive organizations par excellence. They are not businesses in the strict sense of the term, although in some cases their operating budgets may be on a par with Fortune 500 companies.

In the United States, faculty governance is an important concept. Although some people criticize collective governance and there is evidence of corporate culture growing within higher education (Association of Governing Boards, 1996; Carlin, 1999), the idea of self-governance remains a defining principle and nearly inviolable right for most faculty. Along these lines, faculty are akin to partners in a professional practice. Academe tends toward individualism, which poses a significant cultural challenge because knowledge management is predicated on enterprisewide commitment to a common strategy. This may be a difficult norm to establish in university environments (and certainly in some corporate environments too), yet there are compelling reasons that universities should be interested in applying knowledge management to their operational activities. With public sector support declining and competition for extramural funding increasing, universities need to identify, protect, and exploit their knowledge assets better. They may, for example, emulate consulting firms by marketing proprietary knowledge. A group of faculty in the United Kingdom recently formed Knowledge Guru as a vehicle through which to sell their expertise in business and management, travel and tourism, and law

("Dons Become Internet 'Knowledge Gurus,'" 1999). Or universities may choose to repurpose their program offerings, including knowledge management courses, for new or extended markets.

There are three predominant approaches to knowledge management: process engineering, access engineering, and cultural engineering. They are not, of course, mutually exclusive, although each is currently favored or endorsed by a different community of practice. The approaches share a common objective: to transform an organization's capability with various engineering techniques, all of which contribute to effective knowledge management. We examine these approaches in both corporate and university contexts to show points of convergence and divergence.

Process Engineering: Releasing Latent Value

The process engineering approach emphasizes the discovery and extrusion of new knowledge from existing processes and content. A variety of discovery tools and techniques (including process engineering, data mining, yield management software, intelligent agents, neural nets, and recommender systems) can yield useful insight and innovation ("Knowledge Discovery," 1999). For instance, researchers at MIT (Malone and others, 1999) have developed a comprehensive process repository that can provide companies (or universities, for that matter) with interlinked maps of key process types and parts. The process repository can foster creative thinking about new ways to work, and corporations such as Dow Corning are using the tool (Carr, 1999). The process maps, or asset road maps, can be used to identify resources (Macintosh and Stader, 1999) that make matching abilities to tasks more efficient.

Knowledge extraction and pattern matching, two core activities associated with artificial intelligence research and expert system design, lie at the heart of the process approach. Discovering untapped knowledge, codified or experiential, is a key feature of this engineering model. This is as true for academe as business. A good illustration is the series of studies by Swanson and collaborators (for example, Swanson and Smalheiser, 1999) that demonstrates how hidden public knowledge present in related, but not connected, data sets can be illuminated with software designed to create suggestive juxtapositions. From an accounting perspective, the objective is to reveal and capitalize on hidden assets.

Universities can barter and trade expertise and domain knowledge in various markets (Prusak and Cohen, 1997) just as investment bankers bill clients for their knowledge of equities and securities, scholars trade new ideas by e-mail and share research results at conferences, or companies sell portfolios of patents to interested buyers. The ultimate exchange value, or selling price, is affected by such variables as the scarcity, integrity, and uniqueness of the knowledge, along with seller reputation, perceived utility, consumer discrimination, transaction costs, and market transparency.

Often organizations and individuals are unaware of the potential value—in monetary or utility terms—of their knowledge assets. Patents, the focus of *Rembrandts in the Attic* (Rivette and Kline, 1999), provide a particularly good example that crosses a range of sectors and firms, including IBM, Gillette, Dow Chemical, Dell, and Lucent as well as dot-coms such as Amazon (Rivette and Kline, 2000). Thus, a company's true market worth may be multiples of its traditional book value once core competence, reputation, strategic skills sets, brand salience, organizational expertise, intellectual property, proprietary technology, and other factors are taken into account. The challenge for companies is to account for "the potential for future earnings that knowledge creates" (Webber, 1999, p. 222).

Business seems to have realized that traditional accounting measures are inadequate (Hall, 1989). For example, Skandia, a Swedish investment company, has been a notable pioneer in systematically quantifying its intellectual capital base. And its early appointment of a corporate director of intellectual capital sent a strong signal to the business world (Edvinsson and Malone, 1997). In contrast, universities have been slow to change their conceptions of managerial and accounting practices in this regard, and may well be sitting on underexploited and underperforming assets such as prototypes, patents, courseware, specialized faculty expertise, and unique archival collections.

Typical knowledge management strategies for business stress the processes of capturing, exploiting, and protecting institutional expertise. A consulting firm's goal is to enrich the quality of advice and analysis it offers clients and customers by optimizing the array of knowledge assets, such as experience and expertise, at its disposal. But the need to protect those intellectual assets and proprietary techniques that confer a competitive edge is also important. There is a fine line between vaunting one's strengths and exposing one's hand.

The situation is different for universities, however. Here, the construction of knowledge draws on an established set of open practices: the scholarly communication system. At the heart of this process lies peer review. When scholars vet their work for publication, they strive to have their ideas as widely disseminated, discussed, and used as possible, including in the classroom, within their disciplinary communities, and in the public sphere. Consulting firms may not routinely broadcast and share information, but these activities are second nature within the academy.

Competition for attention drives the academic marketplace (Franck, 1999). More than anything else, scholars want their work to stand out from the mass of other publications that compete daily for their peers' attention and approval. This fundamental difference in mission and outlook obviously has a bearing on the approaches to knowledge management favored by the two kinds of organizations. The classic academic norm (for example, free exchange of ideas, unfettered access to information and knowledge, and widespread dissemination of new findings) is not that of the marketplace, where stringent protection and controlled release of proprietary knowledge are commonplace. The differences in communicative cultures between business and traditional academia differ in important aspects, and these differences will have an impact on institutional knowledge management practices and policies.

Access Engineering: The Codification of Content

Historically, the term *knowledge* has referred to codified experience that is gathered, stored, and retrieved from a variety of receptacles. These receptacles, or containers—a physical object, such as a book or paper file in an archive or library, or a virtual repository, such as a database, patent record, or Web site—can be organized and managed according to established documentary conventions, such as tagging, indexing, classifying, and cataloguing. This approach implies process control and content stability. In general terms, the container model seems to work when information can be systematically organized, expertly codified, and widely diffused as, for example, in the formal records of scientific research in scholarly journals. The attempted appropriation of knowledge management by the library and information science (LIS) and other professional groups (such as records and information technology managers) is only to be expected, as knowledge management is viewed as an opportunity to develop professionally and acquire enhanced legitimacy (Rowley, 1999; Schwarzwalder, 1999).

The library profession's attachment to the container metaphor, reinforced by ranking research libraries by collection size, as well as the profession's fondness for "universal description of the world of knowledge" (Davenport and Cronin, 1998, p. 268), may blind it to new models of domain-specific knowledge construction, use, and access at the local level. Knowledge management is not coextensive with the containment and codification model, whether realized in a research library or an expertise querying system (Budzik and Hammond, 1999). The access engineering approach may neglect informal learning, tacit knowledge, sharing, and collaborative learning (Davenport and Cronin, 2000). Incorporated knowl-edge—rules of thumb, savoir faire, expertise—is not easily articu-lated (Callon, 1994). Further, a particular research community's discourse may be so locally grounded and dynamic in character that universal classification schemes will have to be customized (Dav-enport and Cronin, 1998). The long-term consequence of an overly restrictive loyalty to traditional ways of working with information may be that end users go elsewhere for what they need. To under-score this point, consider the conclusions of a recent knowledge management survey sponsored by the Library and Information Ser-vice Commission in the United Kingdom (TFPL Ltd., 1999). This survey revealed that the traditional skills of the LIS community "need to be applied in a new context and linked to business processes and core operations."

Some university librarians understand the general principles of knowledge management and have made strides to provide seamless, off-site access to local and remote resources. Although there is cur-rently greater emphasis on dissemination, we can expect further advances in filtering and personalized profiling. In general, however, librarians are far from developing customized intelligence, or cur-rent awareness, services for their users (Cronin, 1989). Such ser-vices abandon the monolithic view that the library is the gateway to recorded knowledge. Although libraries continue to support the teaching and research missions of the university, they are one of many on- and off-campus supporters. For some scholars and stu-dents, the university library remains the place of first (and last) resort; for others, many of the library's traditional services and facil-ities are unimportant because they rely instead on local or special-ized collections, remote connections, and invisible colleges.

At the interorganizational level, library co-prosperity initiatives and consortia—all quintessential examples of procedural knowledge sharing at the operational level—have been a defining feature for a decade, mirroring the growth of joint ventures, strategic partnerships, and alliances in the corporate world. More and more, information and knowledge resources are being digitized and decentralized, which has both supply-side and demand-side implications—for example, increasing complexity of hybrid collection management and heightened user expectations.

Knowledge management can spawn products in a number of ways. In the course of their work, academics routinely develop new ideas, write books and courseware, develop technologies, and design prototypes with commercial potential. The examples are not always obvious: consider a prize-winning translation of Renaissance writer Francesco Petrarch or the concept for a biotechnology start-up.

Production and licensing of multimedia course materials, an asset base extension, is a growing trend that will likely accelerate with the expansion of distance and distributed education (Cronin, 1998). This version of commodification is characterized, in its extreme form, by separating content from process (design, production, delivery, assessment, distribution, and franchising), similar to business process reengineering in the corporate sector. In this environment, the role of information specialists is to ensure access to the institution's codified knowledge, represented by the library and other knowledge bases that support remote, or perpetual, learning. The role of academic and technical support staff, akin to middle managers in the corporate environment, is to oversee the processes of course production and delivery and ensure they are separated from the faculty, whose task is to transfer knowledge through the curriculum (Davenport and Cronin, 2000; Dolence and Norris, 1995).

On the research and development front, universities are becoming more adept at technology transfer. In fiscal 1997, U.S. universities earned $46 million in royalties and were awarded 2,239 new patents (Basinger, 1999). Start-ups are routinely spun out of the academy, and joint ventures are established with commercial partners in areas such as multimedia design, software engineering, and biotechnology. Many universities now provide seed capital, incubator environments, business advice, and legal guidance to entrepreneurially inclined faculty and researchers. In the United Kingdom, for instance, the government recently earmarked $40 million to establish eight university enterprise centers to encourage scientists to commercialize their ideas (Farrar, 1999).

Some have also suggested ranking universities according to their success in forging links with industry (Tysome, 1999). In the United States, the Lilly Endowment recently made two major awards totaling $60 million ($30 million each to Indiana University and Rose-Hulman Institute) that encourage the link between university-based research and local economic development.

Some universities also manage complex copyright, patent, and licensing agreement portfolios. From a knowledge management perspective, it is strategically important for universities to create mechanisms for institutionalizing the management of distributed intellectual capital. For example, universities need platforms and tools to showcase local expertise and identify possible sources of marketable discoveries, find ideas in need of patent or trademark protection, and capitalize on latent business development opportunities.

Perhaps the most dramatic illustration of knowledge-based valuation has been the recent spate of initial public offerings for virtual corporations (Karlgaard, 1999). High valuations of these companies reflect investors' optimistic belief that intangible assets (for example, a founder's vision, capacity for innovation, high-technology awareness, organizational flexibility, connection to the customer, digital brand salience, trustworthiness) drive business success. Historically, these assets have had no value on the balance sheet. Today, both the public and private sectors recognize the need to develop effective techniques for measuring and exploiting an organization's intellectual capital—human, structural, and customer (Webber, 1999).

Companies that nurture proprietary skills among their employees will be at a distinct advantage in knowledge-intensive markets that have rapid innovation cycles (Stewart, 1997). This point, of course, applies equally to universities, a fact born of fierce competition to attract and retain stars in the U.S. system and by the transfer mania that the Research Assessment Exercise (RAE) has triggered in the United Kingdom. There, institutions are scrambling to attract the most productive faculty in an effort to burnish their research credentials and influence government support for research. The brand-reinforcing and asset-amplifying power of academic superstars make this minority highly valued and highly mobile. Managing these human intellectual capital assets and measuring relative rates of return will be a major challenge for leading higher education institutions.

Cultural Engineering: Leveraging Interaction

The cultural engineering approach poses the strongest challenge to those who manage institutional knowledge. The approach stresses knowing over knowledge and interaction more than outcome. The two previous models viewed knowledge as encoded and embedded in artifacts, structures, systems, and repositories. Knowledge is objectified and quantified. It is something we acquire, accumulate, and use. This building block image of science captures the idea that knowledge structures can be configured just like a building made from Lego® bricks. In contrast, activity theorists emphasize process and emergence, noting that knowledge is situated, provisional, and contested (Blacker, 1995). From this perspective, learning is a dynamic and continuous activity—a process of social construction that is shaped, in part, by prevailing community values, group practices, and institutional norms. As Stein (1995, p. 26) notes, "The processes of social interaction change the structure of the knowledge-base of the organization over time."

This interactional approach shifts the focus from knowledge-qua-knowledge to the continually evolving processes and procedures that promote effective interaction and learning. From a managerial perspective, the question is, What infrastructure needs to be in place to ensure that the necessary stimuli, insights, awareness, and information are available when required? In concrete terms, this might mean developing an enterprise ontology (think of it as a common lexicon) for enhancing cross-unit communication and intraorganizational learning (Usehold and others, 1998). Or it could involve using a balanced scorecard approach, as described by Christopher Peebles (2000; Peebles and others, 1999) in the context of managing a complex university information technology organization. Ultimately, however, it entails creating a space, the academic village reconstituted, in which both tacit and explicit knowledge can be combined and shared by faculty and students alike (Lyman, 1999).

The challenge is to design a customized yet flexible infrastructure that supports both individual and collective learning so the organization, whether a corporation or a university, can adapt to discontinuous change in its operating environment—knowing construed as adaptive coupling. Successful organizations will create the environmental conditions that facilitate the institutionalization of distributed knowledge assets. However, experience tells us that what works in one setting may not prove effective in another. Rob Kling (1999) has shown the importance of contextual inquiry by contrasting the implementations of intranets in two major consulting companies: similar contexts, similar solutions, but quite dissimilar adoption and satisfaction profiles. Knowledge management approaches that overemphasize platforms and productivity tools at the expense of social processes and values in all likelihood will fail to live up to their promise.

A major problem is establishing an appropriate level of aggregation. In both corporate and university environments, there may be tension between the institution as a whole and the specialty group within. Despite growing interdisciplinary research and teaching, specialization and separation remain the norm in most academic fields (Brown and Duguid, 1998). The net effect is fragmentation and intramural isolation. Within and between university departments there may be minimal communication and mutual incomprehension, as the culture and science wars have shown (Gross and Levitt, 1994; Kernan, 1999). Students and faculty may know little, if anything, about the knowledge construction processes outside their own discipline. What constitutes evidence? What warrants belief in other disciplines?

But incommensurability of methods and mutual ignorance, or even intolerance, of worldviews is only part of the problem. Many scholars' primary allegiance is to their field or subfield rather than their parent discipline or institution. And their most substantive professional interactions are often with members of a globally distributed community of practice rather than local colleagues. The sense of community in the contemporary university is somewhat tenuous. Loss of social cohesion and institutional fission can translate into lost opportunity.

From a global asset management perspective, universities in some cases may not be optimizing their human intellectual capital base. Career administrators typically see the world differently from faculty. For them loyalty is localized, and peer institutions are typically viewed less as potential partners than as competitors for federal funds, students, endowments, stellar faculty, and public salience. These cultural differences run deep and will undoubtedly condition receptivity toward knowledge management within different campus constituencies.

Consider that for North American provosts and presidents, the unit evaluated is the department (this is also true in the United Kingdom following the introduction of the RAE). How well is a particular academic department doing? How highly is it ranked? At the departmental level, however, the unit assessed is the individual professor. Merit awards are based on individual accomplishment. In short, there is a structural tension between individual and collective performance assessment. And the picture is more complicated. Multiple tensions exist between institutional, faculty, departmental, specialty group, and individual aims and objectives. Similar tensions can, of course, exist in the consulting world and elsewhere and have been emphasized in sociotechnical studies of intranet adoption (Kling, 1999). For instance, many consultants (and other professionals) do not take kindly to sharing knowledge and pooling expertise for the good of the whole. Nor do they particularly like that annual appraisals take formal account of their contributions to the corporate knowledge base. Such practices constitute a radical shift in organizational culture and the prevailing reward system. What additional resistance might administrators encounter if such practices and policies are imposed on faculty? While it may be difficult to instill a common sense of purpose and a core set of values in a corporate context, it is surely much more so in the sometimes almost anarchic world of the academy, where the idea of business process reengineering is anathema.

Academic cooperation, including human intellectual capital sharing, comes in many guises that range from coauthoring of a grant proposal to organizing tightly structured teams that are a defining feature of the high-energy physics research community. For faculty, connectivity is a crucial factor in stimulating and sustaining local and remote collaboration, which can range from the multilateral exchange of primary data over high-bandwidth networks to collaborative editing of a journal article. The Space Physics and Aeronomy Research Collaboratory, funded by the National Science Foundation, permits space physics researchers worldwide to control and gather data from more than a dozen instruments around the world. The participating researchers also have real-time access to supercomputer models of upper-atmospheric phenomena and an array of communication tools, including chatrooms and a shared whiteboard utility.

Such experimental networks, and their associated augmentation tools, can increase the intensity of scholarly interaction and the velocity of knowledge sharing and discovery, conferring a measure of competitive edge on those involved. Universities that want to develop enhanced knowledge management capability need to recognize that connectivity is not a campus-centric issue. External links are critically important. Because of the nature of big science research, work teams acquire a transinstitutional character. Competing institutions will need to forge partnerships to advance their individual agendas.

The concept of strategic coevolution (Moore, 1996) applies as much to higher education as business and is heavily dependent on internetworking capability—the capacity for networking between organizations. But we should not oversimplify. "Collaboratories" may prove effective for some groups but not for others. Success depends on established work practices within a particular academic discipline, the ease with which trust between participants can be established on-line, and the existence of conventions for information sharing, priority determination, and data ownership (Ross-Flanigan, 1998). To design and implement successful knowledge management, administrators will have to be sensitive to sociocultural contexts and behavioral variables.

Conclusion

None of the broad approaches (process, access, and cultural engineering) sketched in this chapter perfectly defines knowledge management, nor is any one inherently incompatible with the underlying construct. Of the three, however, the interactional position best captures an organization's complexity and flow in the knowledge capitalism age (Burton-Jones, 1999). This method also helps shift attention away from stewarding resources (that is, librarians) to managing contexts in which knowing can occur. Ideally a knowledge management strategy should combine the approaches.

Universities, unlike consulting firms, operate in a highly complex political economy. Audience and mission heterogeneity make it extremely difficult for them to impose standardized solutions across both the academic and administrative hemispheres. In practice, universities are likely to use various approaches to institutionalization, depending on the prevailing circumstances and culture. Initially, at least, knowledge management techniques (for example, departmental and specialty group intranets designed to build awareness of expertise, scholarly resources, and institutional capability) are more likely to be applied selectively, where faculty and administrative buy-in is a reasonable expectation.

In terms of knowledge management, there are significant functional and procedural similarities between corporate and higher education environments (for example, procurement, inventory control, personnel, compliance, marketing, fundraising, and customer service), and lessons learned in the former, such as the value of seeding and nurturing communities of practice (Wenger and Snyder, 2000), should be transferable to the latter. Competition has intensified in both worlds. In both there is a premium on the ability to innovate, foster organizational learning, and engage in double-loop learning—that is, going beyond procedural modification based on feedback analysis to reexamining underlying organizational norms, expectations, and strategies in the light of outcomes (Argyris and Schön, 1978).

Successful organizations will be self-aware and will adapt to their environment. A defining characteristic of such organizations, both universities and consulting firms, will be a commitment to developing a battery of reflection aids (for example, enterprise ontologies, knowledge asset inventories, and knowledge discovery tools) and to creating a culture in which sharing and cooperation are distinguishing characteristics.

References

Argyris, C., and Schön, D. *Organizational Learning: A Theory of Action Perspective*. Reading, Mass.: Addison-Wesley, 1978.

Association of Governing Boards of Universities and Colleges. *The Academic Presidency: Stronger Leadership for Tougher Times*. Washington, D.C.: Association of Governing Boards of Universities and Colleges, 1996.

Basinger, J. "Universities' Royalty Increased 33% in 1997, Reaching $446 Million." *Chronicle of Higher Education*, Jan. 8, 1999, p. A51.

Blacker, F. "Knowledge, Knowledge Work and Organizations: An Overview and Interpretation." *Organization Studies*, 1995, *16*(6), 1021–1046.

Brown, J. S., and Duguid, P. "Organizing Knowledge." *California Management Review*, 1998, *40*(3), 90–111.

Budzik, J., and Hammond, K. "Q and A: A System for the Capture, Organization and Reuse of Expertise." In L. Woods (ed.), *ASIS '99. Proceedings of the 62nd ASIS Annual Meeting. Knowledge: Creation, Organization and Use. Washington, D.C., October 31–November 4, 1999*. Medford, N.J.: Information Today, 1999.

Burton-Jones, A. *Knowledge Capitalism: Business, Work, and Learning in the New Economy*. New York: Oxford University Press, 1999.

Callon, M. "Is Science a Public Good?" *Science, Technology, and Human Values*, 1994, *19*(4), 395–424.

Carlin, J. F. "Restoring Sanity to an Academic World Gone Mad." *Chronicle of Higher Education*, Nov. 5, 1999, p. A76.

Carr, N. G. "A New Way to Manage Process Knowledge." *Harvard Business Review*, Sept.–Oct. 1999, pp. 24–25.

Crainer, S., and Dearlove, D. *Gravy Training: Inside the Business of Business Schools*. San Francisco: Jossey-Bass, 1999.

Cronin, B. "Research Libraries: An Agenda for Change." *British Journal of Academic Librarianship*, 1989, *4*(1), 19–26.

Cronin, B. "The Electronic Academy Revisited." *ASLIB Proceedings*, 1998, *50*(9), 241–254.

Davenport, E., and Cronin, B. "Some Thoughts on 'Just for You' Service in the Context of Domain Expertise." *Journal of Education for Library and Information Science*, 1998, *39*(4), 264–274.

Davenport, E., and Cronin, B. "Knowledge Management: Semantic Drift or Conceptual Shift?" *Journal of Education for Library and Information Science*, 2000, *41*(4).

Dolence, M., and Norris, D. *Transforming Higher Education: A Vision for Learning in the 21st Century*. Ann Arbor, Mich.: Society for College and University Planning, 1995.

"Dons Become Internet 'Knowledge Gurus.'" *Times Higher Education Supplement,* Sept. 17, 1999, p. 2.

Edvinsson, L., and Malone, M. S. *Intellectual Capital: Realizing Your Company's True Value by Finding Its Hidden Brainpower.* New York: HarperCollins, 1997.

Farrar, S. "Cash for Eight Centers of Ideas." *Times Higher Education Supplement,* Sept. 17, 1999, p. 4.

Franck, G. "Scientific Communication—A Vanity Fair?" *Science,* 1999, *286,* 53–54.

Gross, P. R., and Levitt, N. *Higher Superstition: The Academic Left and Its Quarrels with Science.* Baltimore, Md.: Johns Hopkins University Press, 1994.

Hall, R. "The Management of Intellectual Assets: A New Corporate Perspective." *Journal of General Management,* 1989, *15*(1), 53–68.

Karlgaard, R. "Maybe Not So Crazy." *Forbes,* Jan. 25, 1999, p. 43.

Kernan, A. *In Plato's Cave.* New Haven, Conn.: Yale University Press, 1999.

Kling, R. "What Is Social Informatics and Why Does It Matter?" *D-Lib Magazine,* 1999, *5*(1). [www.dlib.org/dlib/january99/kling/01kling.html].

"Knowledge Discovery." A special collection of articles in *Communications of the ACM,* 1999, *42*(11).

Lyman, P. "Designing Libraries to Be Learning Communities: Towards an Ecology of Places for Learning." In S. Criddle, L. Dempsy, and R. Heseltine (eds.), *Information Landscapes for a Learning Society: Networking and the Future of Libraries, 3.* London: Library Association, 1999.

Macintosh, A., and Stader, J. "Knowing Who Knows What—Skills and Capability Ontologies." In *International Symposium on the Management of Industrial and Corporate Knowledge.* ISMICK99 Pre-proceedings. Rotterdam, Netherlands: School of Management of Erasmus University of Rotterdam, 1999.

Malone, T. W., and others. "Tools for Inventing Organizations: Toward a Handbook of Organizational Processes." *Management Science,* 1999, *45*(3), 425–443.

Moore, J. F. *The Death of Competition: Leadership and Strategy in the Age of Business Ecosystems.* New York: HarperBusiness, 1996.

Peebles, C. S. "Lifecycle Costs in Information Technology Include More Than Cost of Hardware." In J. V. Boettcher, M. M. Doyle, and R. W. Jensen (eds.), *Technology-Driven Planning: Principles to Practice.* Ann Arbor, Mich.: Society for College and University Planning, 2000.

Peebles, C. S., and others. "Modeling and Managing the Cost and Quality of Information Technology Services at Indiana University: A Case Study."

In R. N. Katz and J. A. Rudy (eds.), *Information Technology in Higher Education: Assessing Its Impact and Planning for the Future*. San Francisco: Jossey-Bass, 1999.

Prusak, L., and Cohen, D. "Knowledge Buyers, Sellers, and Brokers: The Political Economy of Knowledge." Ernst and Young Center for Business Innovation Working Paper, Jan. 1997.

Rivette, K. G., and Kline, D. *Rembrandts in the Attic: Unlocking the Hidden Value of Patents*. Cambridge, Mass.: Harvard University Press, 1999.

Rivette, K. G., and Kline, D. "Discovering New Value in Intellectual Property." *Harvard Business Review*, 2000, *78*(1), 54–66.

Ross-Flanigan, N. "The Virtues (and Vices) of Virtual Colleagues." [www.techreview.com/articles/ma98/ross-flanigan.html]. 1998.

Rowley, J. "Owners of Knowledge." *Library Association Record*, 1999, *101*(8), 475.

Sarvary, M. "Knowledge Management and Competition in the Consulting Industry." *California Management Review*, 1999, *41*(2), 95–107.

Schwarzwalder, R. "Librarians as Knowledge Management Agents." *Econtent*, 1999, *22*(4), 63–65.

Stein, E. W. "Organizational Memory: Review of Concepts and Recommendations for Management." *International Journal of Information Management*, 1995, *15*(1), 17–32.

Stewart, T. A. *Intellectual Capital: The New Wealth of Organizations*. New York: Currency/Doubleday, 1997.

Swanson, D., and Smalheiser, N. R. "Implicit Text Linkages Between Medline Records: Using Arrowsmith as an Aid to Scientific Discovery." *Library Trends*, 1999, *48*(1), 48–59.

TFPL Ltd. "Skills for Knowledge Management." [www.lic.gov.uk/publications/executivesummaries/kmskills.html]. 1999.

Tysome, T. "League Plan to Attract Firms." *Times Higher Education Supplement*, Dec. 10, 1999, p. 3.

Usehold, M., and others. "The Enterprise Ontology." *Knowledge Engineering Review*, 1998, *13*(1), 31–89.

Webber, A. M. "New Math for a New Economy." *Fast Company*, Jan.–Feb. 1999, pp. 214–224.

Wenger, E. C., and Snyder, W. M. "Communities of Practice: The Organizational Frontier." *Harvard Business Review*, 2000, *78*(1), 139–145.

3

Knowledge Discovery in a Networked World

Peter Lyman

As information technology has transformed the practices of knowledge discovery, the resulting cultural and scientific innovations have shaped the new social environments and institutions that we have begun to call the information society and the knowledge economy. It is not surprising that academic research, the source of many of these new technologies, is deeply engaged in this remarkable cycle of invention and organizational innovation. Thus, it seems paradoxical that colleges and universities, historic centers for knowledge discovery, have been reluctant to use information technology for organizational innovation or to seek new relationships to a society and economy that increasingly seems to value learning and research.

Knowledge management offers higher education a framework for planning and managing the innovation now being driven by information technologies, yet the very idea of *managing* knowledge seems to contradict the basic principles of academic governance.

At the core of academic culture is the belief that higher education should be administered, not managed. Like other important words in higher education—*profession, vocation, office, discipline, information, tutor* (and, by extension, *tuition*)—the word *administration* had a sacred connotation in the medieval university: to minister, serve, steward, execute an office, and in general act as a guardian or custodian (Chodorow and Lyman, 1998). In contrast to the delegated and limited authority of administration, the word *management* originally connoted training (for example, of horses), but in the past century it has evolved into a command-and-control paradigm that has seemed inappropriate for academic organizations. Academic administrators might *manage* staff or infrastructure, but knowledge discovery—research and learning—should be *administered*. Knowledge management, however, is a concept rooted in business practices that are optimized for research and development and thus might be consonant with academic values.

The need for a new paradigm to manage innovation in academe is urgent. Neither management nor administration can solve the problems that higher education now faces. Some of these problems are external, such as new intellectual property laws, competition by e-commerce and biotechnology for the best minds, and the increasingly permeable boundaries between academic and commercial research. And some of these problems are internal, such as the fiscal crisis in the system of scholarly publishing, the difficulty in developing standards for electronic publishing and learning technologies, and the rise of collaborative research that crosses institutional, national, and disciplinary borders. All can be traced back to a remarkable process of economic innovation stimulated by information technology, making the inability of higher education to manage innovation in its organizational structure and pedagogy even more striking.

Information technology (IT) does not inevitably lead to innovation. In the first phase, IT was applied to the automation of routine processes and management of data to increase efficiency and control quality. Next, business systems were optimized for information management and applied to problems such as inventory and personnel management. UNIX architecture developed to support collaborative scientific research, using IT for instrumentation, analysis, visualization, and communication. But it is the Internet, initially conceived as an information superhighway between computers, that has placed the focus on knowledge. The knowledge management paradigm arose to deal with the business innovations that followed: just-in-time production managed by electronic data interchange (EDI); disintermediation, linking customers directly to suppliers; and the new networked corporation defined by the production, ownership, and management of intellectual capital (Castells, 1996).

Knowledge management grew out of the recognition that the knowledge of employees—tacit knowledge, expertise, and explicit information—is a strategic resource in a knowledge economy (Brown and Duguid, 1998). And indeed, the academic world is organized around a similar recognition: a faculty is defined by the practice of a discipline of knowledge discovery, as, for example, the faculty of arts and sciences. Thus, the issues facing higher education are precisely those that knowledge management has been developing new concepts and techniques to solve. Given that IT poses unrealized opportunities for higher education that knowledge management might help to attain, this chapter addresses the following three questions:

1. *Why is higher education a leader in invention but slow to use the network to create innovative new modes of teaching and learning, research, and service?* Information is ubiquitous in every aspect of educational institutions—the library, classrooms, and laboratories—yet is often treated as an infrastructure to be managed rather than as a strategic resource. To this end, knowledge management offers thought-provoking concepts such as the virtual enterprise and the productivity paradox, and proposes the establishment of a new management role to manage innovation: the chief knowledge officer (CKO).

2. *What is the future of the knowledge management services provided by learned societies?* Scholarly publication and disciplinary meetings

have been the currency of knowledge discovery within the academic community, linking researchers who are geographically distributed as departmental faculty in educational institutions. Today the network offers a new form of publication and virtual meeting spaces for disciplines. Here knowledge management offers the concept of communities of practice to think about the social and cultural dimensions of knowledge discovery in a networked world.

3. *Who owns the rights to the processes and products of knowledge discovery?* Scholarly communication was originally the province of learned societies, has been commercialized by multinational publishers over the past fifty years, and is now evolving into digital library e-commerce services protected by intellectual property law. Here knowledge management offers the concept of information flows and differentiates business models in a manner that may help to clarify the collaborative possibilities offered by networked social spaces.

To explore these questions, this chapter begins by addressing the management of digital technologies, comparing the chief knowledge officer in business to the campus chief information officer or director of academic computing. It then describes how the network is changing the process and practice of knowledge discovery and the implications of on-line communities of practice for the traditional modes of scholarly publishing that have defined academic disciplines in the past; reviews the relevance of e-commerce business strategies for higher education; and explores the relationship between higher education and other knowledge industries.

Managing the Network Infrastructure

Knowledge management began with Peter Drucker's (1978) observation that in the twentieth century, management focused on the productivity of manual labor, but in the twenty-first century, management must focus on the productivity of knowledge workers. What can knowledge management tell us, then, about the impact of campus information technologies on the productivity of researchers, teachers, and learners?

Scholarly literature on the impact of digital networks is very new, but three interrelated findings might help to focus campus planning concerning the strategic goals and objectives of information technology:

Efficiency. IT is often introduced to increase efficiency, but is more likely to change the quality of work by changing its processes and outputs (Zuboff, 1984). Computation itself is important in knowledge discovery—as instrumentation for data collection, visualization, data management, data mining, and so forth—but these bear on the quality of research more than the productivity of the researcher.

Productivity. A complex debate referred to as the productivity paradox asks why the introduction of information technology has not seemed to increase the productivity of knowledge workers. The simple answer is that the introduction of IT itself does not produce innovation, for productivity increases require significant redefinition of the measurement and valuation of work outcomes, the creation of new cultures of work, and the reorganization of work processes (Brynjolfsson, 1993). This is certainly the case in higher education, where IT is ubiquitous, but organizational and cultural change proceeds at glacial speeds (Massy and Zemsky, 1995; Lyman, 1999).

Innovation. The innovation process is difficult to manage because users often drive innovation in unexpected directions. François Bar's study of the impact of intranets on corporations found that in the first two years, data management (that is, inventory control, personnel records, and so forth) is 80 percent of intranet use. In subsequent years, data management usage levels out, while user-driven collaborative work grows to 80 percent of usage (Bar, Kane, and Simard, 2000; Bar and Riis, 2000). In practice, then, information management ultimately implies knowledge management, because networks change social relationships and thereby the content of research.

Rather than follow these tempting footnote trails into the literature of technology and innovation, it is more useful to illustrate these findings by describing what chief knowledge officers (CKOs) do in corporations. Two recent surveys of CKO work help to illustrate the practice of knowledge management (Ruggles, 1998; Earl and Scott, 1999).

Networks are the key infrastructure because they create organizational flexibility. Intranets are installed to support collaborative work; extranets are a medium for business-to-business (B-to-B) coordination and business-to-customer (B-to-C) e-commerce. Thus, knowledge management does not define knowledge workers in terms of their organizational roles, but as nodes of expertise that are resources that might be connected in new patterns to solve new problems. Data warehouses provide broad organizational context to what is known by individual knowledge workers, and decision support tools are introduced, including databases that identify the expertise and best practices of others across the organization. Most important, networks are seen as organizational tools; groupware and computer-supported collaborative work systems are implemented to support work among people who may be geographically distant from each other. (Information about this rapidly evolving technology is available from the Association for Computing Machinery Conference on Information and Knowledge Management at www.cs.umbc.edu/cikm/.)

One of the main themes of knowledge management is support of virtual organizations on the network, variously called computer-supported collaborative work (CSCW), groupware, virtual communities, network enterprises, collaboratories, and communities of practice. Implicitly, then, the goal of knowledge management is not to use IT as a tactical means to increase the efficiency of traditional organizations but to replace those organizations with communication webs that support geographically dispersed groups that are functionally self-governing.

Given this mandate for change within traditional organizations, the modes of authority of the CKO are necessarily contextual: the management of technology, the administration of information, leadership of strategic planning, and, in all contexts, persuasion.

It would be worthwhile to explore if and when corporate CKOs are successful in achieving these knowledge management objectives. However, for our purposes, it is sufficient to note that for all its investment in IT and information, higher education has not yet conceived of such a role, for it does not value these objectives. CIOs, librarians, and directors of academic computing in higher education do not have the authority to manage academic knowledge, treat organization as a variable, or provide leadership for strategic planning (Fleit, 1989). This is a consequence of defining knowledge management as a faculty prerogative centered on the curriculum and research, which has the consequence of reducing campus information technology to an infrastructure management problem. As a consequence, there is no organizational focus for strategic planning related to the network as a communications medium with the potential to produce innovation. New administrative systems are treated as tactical means to increase managerial control, and the unanticipated benefits that the private sector has found so valuable, such as user-driven innovation, organizational flexibility, cost control, and productivity, are unrealized. There are other costs as well, because the abilities of staff knowledge workers without faculty status are not treated as an institutional resource.

Institutional management of knowledge is focused at the margins of the academic enterprise, as when faculty recruitment and retention drive investment in laboratories or a research discovery drives the need for a patent licensing policy. While innovation is an important issue in the research domain, locally innovation is driven by faculty and takes strategic direction from funding agencies such as the National Science Foundation and intellectual direction from disciplinary publications and meetings.

Because these kinds of strategic issues are grounded in quite specific and unique institutional histories and missions, knowledge management cannot provide generic answers. It might, however, provide productive questions for planners about the strategic role of information technologies in higher education:

- *What is the impact of information technologies on the different kinds of knowledge discovery within an institution?* Universities are complex institutions, reflecting very different cultures of knowledge discovery that characterize the disciplines, professions, and arts. In some fields, shared methodology or technique generates a canon; in others, technique seems to be driven by theory. Moreover, within each faculty, different modes of knowledge discovery are applied to research, teaching and learning, and public service. Given this complexity, where is the balance between applications optimized for one discipline and institutional economies of scale?

- *Is organizational innovation a goal?* Higher education is optimized to create and disseminate knowledge, but most higher education organizations have not been subject to strategic planning, experimentation, and change for decades. If organizational innovation were to become a goal, what kind of managerial roles and authority would be required?

- *How would higher education change if staff were defined as knowledge workers?* Knowledge management is focused on the way knowledge is embedded in nearly all work, products, and services, not simply in the research function. The work of the CKO is to develop systems to enhance the productivity and creativity of all knowledge workers.

Managing Scholarly Communication

At the turn of the twentieth century, the modern structure of disciplinary communication and governance was founded, linking faculty across the nation into academic communities through professional meetings and the publication of scholarly journals and monographs. Scholarly publishing has been the approved form of knowledge management for a century, making tacit knowledge explicit through the rhetorical rules of the scientific article and transferring knowledge through the establishment of the research library system for the organization and preservation of scholarly literatures (Brown and Duguid, 2000). Thus, knowledge management has always existed within higher education, but as the responsibility of faculty at the local level and learned societies at the national level. Institutions have subsidized this structure through higher pricing for library journal subscriptions and faculty travel, giving copyrights to scholarly publications, and receiving back peer review quality control useful for promotion and tenure.

At the turn of the twenty-first century, scholarly publishing is evolving into a global system of scholarly communication on the Web, including a spectacular array of multimedia texts based on visualization and real-time network communication. This evolution is still experimental but must be recognized as a collaborative knowledge management project by faculty innovators. It is striking that neither universities nor learned societies are prepared to sustain this work or to recognize it as a strategic opportunity to break the monopoly power of commercial publishers.

Journals allowed for the exchange of information among researchers at different institutions, creating academic communities that the knowledge management literature would call communities of practice. This term originally described the way we learn from working collaboratively within the social contexts that we find at work, because learning comes from both explicit and tacit apprenticeship relationships to others (Lave and Wenger, 1991). One review of the literature describes communities of practice ranging "from the effectiveness of the invisible colleges in the progress of the scientific enterprise, to the roles of cliques in the functioning of bureaucracies. In between, they run the gamut from informal networks of cooperation among chemists working for competitive pharmaceutical industries, to back channel exchanges between members of the foreign offices of adversary countries and the appearance of gangs in schools and prisons" (Huberman and Hogg, 1995, p. 73). Today the term is used to describe collaborative work among members of global scientific and research communities using the Internet.

A particularly striking passage in the knowledge management literature that describes collaborative research in biotechnology raises the key questions about the management of knowledge discovery:

> *The complexity and rapid pace of research means that advances are necessarily made by large teams connected by their interlocking areas of expertise rather than by employment at the same institution or location.* Thus . . . a recently published paper on the DNA sequence of yeast chromosomes listed 133 authors from 85 institutions. . . . These virtual teams point to the future shape of knowledge work in general, which some predict will be accomplished by widely dispersed groups and individuals woven into communities of practice by networks, groupware, and a complex common task. [Cohen, 1998, p. 37, italics added]

Because computer networks enable such communication on an unprecedented scale, the idea of communities of practice is rapidly becoming the foundation for theories of virtual organization, particularly in the literature on the corporation of the future. Thus, one of the important tasks of the CKO is providing information environments that enable communities of practice to take form as needed among employees located anywhere in the world.

Information technology is causing a number of important paradigm shifts in knowledge discovery, reflecting this basic sociological shift from the researcher working in a lab in a given geographical location to real-time collaborative work on the network. The Center for Research on Electronic Work at the University of Michigan describes these technology-based communities of practice as collaboratories (see crew.umich.edu). Instrumentation creates public collections of data, ranging from weather to economic transactions, which are mined by collaboratories, virtual laboratories on the Internet linking researchers all over the world.

The new modes of networked knowledge discovery often are tied directly to data sources or visualize them in interactive ways that may be different for different readers at different points in time. Data mining transforms the relationship between knowledge, the literature, and ownership: data are public, not private; value is added by analysis or context but may be proprietary rather than public; and publication may take the form of software or a contribution to the data set, not a discrete published article. Even so, data mining is becoming a major new research paradigm, although it differs from the traditional currencies of scientific publication and academic credit.

In specific disciplines, the network is creating new forms of publication with revolutionary implications for research, teaching, and service. The relationship between narrative explanation and evidence shifts when evidence is in the public domain first, as in data mining, or when publication is directly linked to evidence, as in multivalent documents. In archeology, for example, technology can support databases containing information about a particular site as a shared resource for the entire profession and with an appropriate front end as a learning tool for students. Thus, the Cotsen Institute of Archeology at the University of California at Los Angeles has organized the

Working Group on Digital Publishing in Archeology to define disciplinary standards and best practices for what is called "the Digital Imprint" (see www.sscnet.ucla.edu/ioa/labs/digital/imprint/proposal .html).

These changes in the knowledge discovery process have fundamental but as yet unaddressed implications for higher education. New forms of scientific research might be superior records of the discovery process, but they may not easily satisfy organizational requirements that research be rank-ordered for promotion and tenure decisions. Who is the author when the literature is collaborative (Biagioli, 1998; Powell, 1998)? What is a publication when the product is part of a database that evolves in real time as research progresses, unlike traditional forms of scholarly publication that freeze the research process into a moment in time (Latour, 1986)?

Higher education has used these problems as reasons not to recognize electronic publication as equal to print publication in tenure and promotion decisions rather than working with learned societies to create a new architecture for disciplinary knowledge management. As we shall see, e-commerce consists of precisely this kind of transformation of the organization, making the network the focal point of transactions, often focused on information services in ways that might provide sustainable business models for new forms of scholarly publishing.

These new models pose problems as well. One constraint on the development of a new architecture for disciplinary knowledge will be intellectual property law. For the past century, higher education has exchanged knowledge through a gift culture subsidized by research libraries, but changes in the intellectual property regime are optimized for a pay-per-view, e-commerce system of document delivery. We return to this environmental constraint in the last section of this chapter.

The strategic agenda for higher education is not defined by competition from e-commerce; it is posed from within in the use of computation, networks, and the Web by researchers who are creating entirely new modes of representation. The problem is that while the current system of scholarly publishing is fatally wounded because it is financially unsustainable (Hawkins, 1998), the new system is still experimental. Thus, the strategic agenda for higher education is urgent, including these questions:

• *How can experimentation with new modes of scholarly communication on the network become cumulative and its technical and rhetorical standards optimized for the needs of the various disciplines and professions?* While significant technological experimentation has been funded by the National Science Foundation's digital library project, those projects are driven by computer science rather than grounded in the specific needs and requirements of various disciplines, and they do not address the issue of economic sustainability. Local innovation is often driven by institutional funding for faculty projects, but it generally does not include operational funds and often cannot be scaled to serve global communities of practice. Moreover, experimentation has yet to produce a critical mass of publication in any given field sufficient to establish standards and disciplinary acceptance.

• *What business model will support scholarly publishing?* It is fundamentally important to recognize that in most fields, the print model of scholarly publication and research libraries is not sustainable. Libraries are not being provided funding to meet sustained high inflation rates in the price of journals, and the market for scholarly monographs has declined to the point that publishers are increasingly unwilling to publish them. Thus, the choice at hand is not print versus digital; it is whether information access will be based on subsidy or fee-for-service e-commerce.

• *What kind of quality control is applicable to collaborative work and network publication for tenure and promotion decisions?* Given answers to the previous two questions, traditional personnel process and criteria might be adapted to new modes of knowledge discovery. But e-commerce suggests an alternative: that demand should become the criterion for valuing publications. This is already implicit in the use of citation indexes, but because on-line usage is easily tracked, this is a policy question more than a technical problem.

• *What organizational strategies should higher education adopt to solve knowledge management problems requiring institutional collaboration?* Perhaps these questions cannot be answered by individual institutions, for lack of scale, if not will, or by learned societies, for lack of resources, if not authority. Invention can be local, but innovation requires coordination and leadership. In the past, there have been similar architectonic moments in the history of American higher education, such as the founding of land grant universities in the nineteenth century and of new disciplines and university presses in the twentieth century. In the past, institutional leaders, such as Harvard's Charles William Eliot and Chicago's Robert Maynard Hutchins, have transcended the administrative mode of academic governance to address strategic issues. Where is that strategic leadership today?

• *Do today's pedagogy and curriculum properly prepare students to work in a knowledge economy?* Teaching and learning are at the heart of the educational enterprise; thus, debates about the role of networks in training and the transfer of skills or tacit knowledge ought to be of interest to higher education. To what extent can the tacit dimensions of knowledge discovery—the arts and skills that are learned by example, by mentoring, and by apprenticeship—be transformed into explicit information, or taught and learned through networked virtual organizations? How well do today's classrooms accomplish these objectives?

Managing Institutional Boundaries

In the past, higher education has been able to differentiate itself from other industries by virtue of a tacit monopoly on education and accreditation. Ironically, the growth of the knowledge economy has made management of the boundary between education and markets far more difficult. One manifestation of this is the issue of ownership of patents and copyrights for the products of faculty research, which is an even more difficult problem when faculty members serve as consultants to industry. Faculty are not simply employees; thus, the rights and duties of faculty have become more ambiguous.

The issue of boundaries has been focused on protecting the current organizational forms of higher education, not the opportunities to develop new organizational forms for lifelong education that might reach into the workplace or the danger of competition from commercial training and development. The opportunity is suggested by Silicon Valley's vision of the future: search engines replacing libraries, virtual organizations replacing bricks and mortar, and global information flows crossing national boundaries. Is this also a vision of the future of higher education?

Paper documents have defined the boundaries of organizations for nearly half a millennium: bureaucracies manage records; business is built on double-entry bookkeeping; and markets are made possible by currencies, science by journals. Knowledge management does not propose that institutions based on paper documents can or should be managed more efficiently with digital documents. It begins with the more radical proposition that networked communication is as stable a foundation for institutions as physical places, face-to-face meetings, or paper documents.

Is this true? Sociologists analyze information technologies as an extension of the process of social innovation begun by industrial technologies. Thus, Karen Cerulo observes, "Like the railroad and the telegraph, the new technologies have redefined space, place and time." And yet, she continues, "technology has provided us with new sites of empirical experience and it has re-configured the complex ties that bind the social and cognitive worlds." Specifically, shared physical presence is no longer the only way in which a sense of social place may be created. "Physical co-presence," she argues, can no longer be the standard "by which to judge the importance, the form, and the quality of all other varieties of exchange" (Cerulo, 1997, pp. 48, 55, 49).

Following from this postulate, Japanese management theorists have argued that the sense of place provided by shared geography may also be sustained by networked communication, shared culture or training, or, most likely, a combination of these factors (Nonaka and Takeuchi, 1995). One school of thought argues that this might be because social networks on the Web are not very different from the social networks found everywhere else in urban society (Wellman and Gulia, 1999). Virtual community and real life are not opposites, for the most durable sense of community develops when people engage in both networked and face-to-face meetings (Virnoche and Marx, 1997).

Manuel Castells describes the virtual corporation as the owner of intellectual capital by which it manages global information flows, outsourcing, and production coordination. Thus, the form and dynamics of the organization change: "What is distinctive to the configuration of the new technological paradigm is its ability to reconfigure, a decisive feature in a society characterized by constant change and organizational fluidity. Turning the rules upside down without destroying the organization has become a possibility, because the material basis of the organization can be reprogrammed and retooled" (Castells, 1996, p. 62). At the heart of Castells's theory is a historic change in the relationship between information and the economy: "The contemporary change of paradigm may be seen as a shift from a technology based primarily on cheap inputs of energy to one predominantly based on cheap inputs of information derived from advances in microelectronic and telecommunications technology. . . . Information is its raw material: these are technologies to act on information, not just information to act on technology, as was the case in previous technological revolutions" (Castells, 1996, p. 67).

Fordism attempted to design knowledge into the technology in order to minimize the need for training. In Shoshana Zuboff's

(1984) phrase, modern production is *informated;* thus, the expertise of the worker becomes a knowledge asset for the corporation. The problem is that the knowledge of employees is at the same time potential intellectual property and an essentially private mental faculty that is difficult to codify and manage. As many organizations have said of themselves, "If we only knew what we know," and this has become the mantra of knowledge management (O'Dell and Grayson, 1998).

The dot-com world consists of the invention of architectures to support virtual social institutions. Business-to-business electronic data interchange (EDI) has made possible the deconstruction of the corporation into the management of information flows supporting just-in-time delivery among global suppliers and customers. In microcosm, librarians in some corporations are now assigned to manage information flows within virtual research discovery collaboratories spread around the world.

Business-to-customer relationships (retail e-commerce) are based on establishing virtual community relationships with customers by customizing portal information through collaborative filtering (Hagel and Armstrong, 1997). The Web has become the information resource of first resort, but the question is how to make it a knowledge resource. Thus, new technologies like Extensible Markup Language (XML) are driving B-to-C commerce, focused on building social relationships by customizing and personalizing information.

Customer-to-customer (C-to-C) dot-com sites, such as eBay's auction site, make possible exchange among people who meet only virtually. This technology supports not only auctions but also virtual communities, or exchange of goods outside the market by barter.

The implication of this argument, if true, is that higher education is addressing the wrong information problem. The problem is not how to digitize libraries to deliver information to the desktop and laboratory; the problem is how to create flexible organizations that reach beyond the boundaries of the physical campus.

MIT has begun to explore whether e-commerce might provide heuristic models for addressing strategic questions about alternative organizational models. Following that lead, we might explore some new options:

- *Education-to-education (E-to-E) cooperation.* On the model of B-to-B communication, what kind of information infrastructure should link institutions of higher education? If we are competitors in some respects, knowledge management requires us to be collaborators as well in order to solve the scholarly communication crisis. B-to-B e-commerce is an infrastructure of standards for EDI that can support shared resources and specialization. For higher education, such standards might address the new architecture for scholarly communications, as well as technical standards for the sharing of distance education courses or educational software. Without them, there are no economies of scale, indeed no markets, for if every technology implementation is experimental, none is sustainable. This infrastructure, of course, is only a means; the more difficult problem is the discovery that strategic problems require collaborative solutions and the will to innovate.

- *Education-to-learner (E-to-L).* Should the physical plant or the people whose names are contained within the campus information systems define the boundaries of the campus? Or should the sense of academic community become more inclusive, using network architectures to include parents, prospective students, alumni, and community? An E-to-L architecture would not only make campus education accessible to distant audiences, it would make educational moments outside the campus accessible to students and faculty.

- *Learner-to-learner (L-to-L).* Like broadcasting, higher education has viewed learning as a matter of receiving information rather than a matter of participating in knowledge discovery. C-to-C technologies are participatory, are capable of supporting communities, and extend learning. What is the role of C-to-C technology in pro-moting deliberative, and therefore self-governing, learning com-munities crossing physical and social boundaries, such as alumni to student or faculty to parent?

One Knowledge Industry Among Many

Perhaps higher education was the first knowledge economy, but it is no longer the only one. In looking at higher education as one knowledge industry among many and the emphasis on learning communities now growing in places other than the academic com-munity, we might find new perspectives on the questions explored in this chapter. Such an experiment quickly yields two difficult final questions.

First, *what will be the impact of the intellectual property revolution on higher education?* Intellectual property law is important for knowl-edge discovery in higher education because it defines the legal rules for the production of information (Benkler, 1999). The new intel-lectual property regime governing digital information does not include the special rights and privileges that higher education has historically enjoyed, such as fair use of copyrighted material, for it is optimized for media industries that intend to privatize educational information. Intellectual property law defines the architecture of knowledge discovery, yet often has been relegated to the status of a library management problem.

Second, *where is organizational innovation in higher education?* While it is easy to exaggerate the relative size and importance of the new economy, it is striking that traditional industries have also placed high priority on exploring the use of information technology to produce organizational innovation. Why isn't higher education more systematic in its use of technology for teaching and learning? Why isn't it more concerned about learning beyond the campus— in the schools, about lifelong learning, for corporate training?

Intellectual Property

At one level, higher education has long since recognized that the knowledge economy has made the boundaries with corporations permeable. Corporate research now draws on faculty consultants in ways that create ambiguity about the ownership of research discoveries. Who owns patent rights for inventions, software, and genetic discoveries produced by faculty research, or the copyright of teaching products created by faculty but marketed outside the university? What will be the impact on scholarly communication of proprietary research protected by corporations as trade secrets, and thus not peer reviewed?

The issues also take more immediate operational forms. For example, the Digital Millennium Copyright Act (DMCA) of 1998 created liabilities and safe harbors that require campuses acting as on-line service providers (for example, providing network services to the campus community) to ensure that copyright law is not violated. It does so by placing liability where there are resources—at the institutional level—and by making the institution responsible for the actions of faculty and graduate assistants. These environmental changes are forcing higher education to rethink the boundaries that differentiate it from business and society. Very good examples of the new management are the DMCA Agent at the University of Chicago (see www.uchicago.edu/uchi/dmcagent.html) and the University of California's *Guidelines for Compliance with the On-line Service Provider Provisions of the Digital Millennium Copyright Act* (see www.ucop.edu/ucophome/coordrev/policy/12-01-99.html).

The intellectual property issue requires us to think about higher education as a knowledge discovery industry with vital stakes in political decisions about intellectual property, the information infrastructure, and innovation policy. Yet it is an industry that has been unable or unwilling to represent its interests in political decision making. Because this industry is so decentralized, each institution is tempted to believe that it can survive unchanged although others may not.

Where Is the Innovation?

Innovation in the organization of higher education occurs at the margins, which seems to be a pattern among complacent industries. In rich institutions, organizational and pedagogical innovation occurs in new markets such as distance education, lifelong education, or residential education—enterprises that must be innovative because they are market-driven businesses. It occurs in professional schools because graduates must be qualified to work for innovative employers. Similarly, community colleges are innovative in applying technology to teaching and learning because they must be responsive to the educational needs of their environments, although they lack the resources and scale to establish new standards and practices. Innovation occurs in research. But innovation has yet to become a strategic priority for the institution as a whole. This raises the political question of whether higher education as now configured will be able to meet the educational needs of the changing society that provides its support.

Perhaps in this context it is useful to remember that in 1940, the highest capitalized firm on the New York Stock Exchange was Baldwin Locomotive, and that the lesson of the market is that industries that do not innovate do not survive. The knowledge management paradigm is, among other things, based on the diagnosis that when institutions like higher education face more organizational anomalies than they can manage, they are facing the kind of historical crisis of innovation that requires returning to fundamental questions.

References

Bar, F., Kane, N., and Simard, C. "Digital Networks and Organizational Change: The Evolutionary Deployment of Corporate Information Infrastructure." Paper presented at the International Sunbelt Social Network Conference, Vancouver, Canada, Apr. 13–16, 2000.

Bar, F., and Riis, A. M. "Tapping User-Driven Innovation: A New Rationale for Universal Service." *Information Society*, 2000, 16, 1–10.

Benkler, Y. "Intellectual Property and the Organization of Information Production." Working draft, Oct. 1999. [www.law.nyu.edu/benklery/Ipec.PDF].

Biagioli, M. "The Instability of Authorship: Credit and Responsibility in Contemporary Biomedicine." *FASEB Journal*, 1998, *12*, 3–16.

Brown, J. S., and Duguid, P. "Organizing Knowledge." *California Management Review*, 1998, *40*(3), 90–111.

Brown, J. S., and Duguid, P. *The Social Life of Information*. Cambridge, Mass.: Harvard Business School Press, 2000.

Brynjolfsson, E. "The Productivity Paradox of Information Technology." *Communications of the ACM*, 1993, *36*(12), 67–77.

Castells, M. *The Network Society*. Oxford, England: Blackwell, 1996.

Cerulo, K. A. "Reframing Sociological Concepts for a Brave New (Virtual?) World." *Sociological Inquiry*, 1997, *67*, 48–58.

Chodorow, S., and Lyman, P. "Challenges to and Responsibilities of Universities in the New Information Environments." In B. Hawkins and P. Battin (eds.), *The Mirage of Continuity: Reconfiguring Academic Information Resources for the 21st Century*. Washington, D.C.: Council on Library and Information Resources and the Association of American Universities, 1998.

Cohen, D. "Toward a Knowledge Context: Report on the First Annual U.C. Berkeley Forum on Knowledge and the Firm." *California Management Review*, 1998, *40*, 22–39.

Drucker, P. F. *The Age of Discontinuity*. New York: HarperCollins, 1978.

Earl, M. J., and Scott, I. A. "The Chief Knowledge Officer: A New Corporate Role." *Sloan Management Review*, 1999, *40*(2), 29–38, 113, 114.

Fleit, L. H. "The Myth of the Computer Czar—Revisited." In B. L. Hawkins (ed.), *Organizing and Managing Information Resources on Campus*. McKinney, Tex.: Academic Computing Publications, 1989.

Hagel, J., III, and Armstrong, A. G. *NetGain*. Cambridge, Mass.: Harvard Business School Press, 1997.

Hawkins, B. "The Unsustainability of the Traditional Library and the Threat to Higher Education." In B. Hawkins and P. Battin (eds.), *The Mirage of Continuity: Reconfiguring Academic Information Resources for the 21st Century*. Washington, D.C.: Council on Library and Information Resources and Association of American Universities, 1998.

Huberman, B. A., and Hogg, T. "Communities of Practice: Performance and Evolution." *Computational and Mathematical Organization Theory*, 1995, *1*, 1.

Latour, B. *Laboratory Life: The Construction of Scientific Facts*. Princeton, N.J.: Princeton University Press, 1986.

Lave, J., and Wenger, E. *Situated Learning: Legitimate Peripheral Participation.* New York: Cambridge University Press, 1991.

Lyman, P. "Digital Documents and the Future of the Academic Community." In R. Ekman and R. E. Quandt (eds.), *Technology and Scholarly Communication.* Berkeley: University of California Press, 1999.

Massy, W. F., and Zemsky, R. "Using Information Technology to Enhance Academic Productivity." White paper from the June 1995 Educom National Learning Infrastructure Initiative (NLII) Roundtable. [www.educause.edu/nlii/keydocs/massy.html].

Nonaka, I., and Takeuchi, H. *The Knowledge-Creating Company.* New York: Oxford University Press, 1995.

O'Dell, C., and Grayson, C. J., Jr. "If Only We Knew What We Know: Identification and Transfer of Internal Best Practices." *California Management Review,* 1998, *40*(3), 154–174.

Powell, W. W. "Learning from Collaboration: Knowledge and Networks in the Biotechnology and Pharmaceutical Industries." *California Management Review,* 1998, *40*, 228–240.

Ruggles, R. "The State of the Notion: Knowledge Management in Practice." *California Management Review,* 1998, *40*, 80–89.

Virnoche, M. E., and Marx, G. T. "'Only Connect'—E. M. Forster in an Age of Electronic Communication: Computer-Mediated Association and Community Networks." *Sociological Inquiry,* 1997, *67*, 85–100.

Wellman, B., and Gulia, M. "Net Surfers Don't Ride Alone: Virtual Communities as Communities." In B. Wellman (ed.), *Networks in the Global Village.* Boulder, Colo.: Westview Press, 1999.

Zuboff, S. *In the Age of the Smart Machine.* New York: Basic Books, 1984.

4

Databases, Information Architecture, and Knowledge Discovery

Patricia M. Wallace, Donald R. Riley

A new gold rush is on as many educational leaders realize how valuable their mountains of digitized data can be—and that these accumulations grow exponentially each year. Most institutions now have one to two decades of computerized information, and the types of data have expanded dramatically. Not only are we flush with digitized student records, personnel information, and financial data, we are now accumulating reams of e-mail, Internet access patterns, course evaluations, documents, marketing statistics, library catalogues, and much more in such diverse storage areas as Web sites and personal digital assistants. In addition to searchable stores, organizational knowledge can also reside in sites that are not digitized, such as people's heads, filing cabinets, and scratch pads.

These rich and ever-growing data sources have raised expectations about how we can use data to create knowledge and make smarter decisions, ones that are based on more accurate and timely information than anything we have ever before been able to assemble. The widespread availability of user-friendly software that can sift data and create meaningful and useful knowledge from them has fueled expectations. Yet despite the flood of data and tools, people get frustrated because these riches seem so difficult to tap.

This chapter explores the technology side of knowledge discovery, focusing on the challenges and opportunities involved in extracting knowledge and getting to the gold in those hills. Terms such as *data mining, decision support,* and *knowledge discovery,* although not clearly defined, reflect our interest in taking better advantage of the available data. From an organizational perspective, it would be advantageous if we "knew what we know" (O'Dell and Grayson, 1998), and technological innovations will certainly help. To understand the challenges involved in knowledge discovery, we begin with a brief discussion of the hills themselves—an organization's information architecture (Cook, 1996).

Information Architectures in Higher Education

An organization's information architecture is a high-level blueprint of its underlying information resources and requirements, which include its hardware, software, data, networks, and the people who maintain and develop these resources. In the early days of computerization, this blueprint was fairly easy for managers to grasp because it was built around a central mainframe. In the mid-1960s, institutions began installing data centers with large host computers that delivered all the computational power to desktop dumb terminals. The emphasis for applications was on operational systems that could keep accurate records of accounts, student registrations, grades, transcripts, class scheduling, and other transactions.

The student information and other systems developed to run on these mainframes were workhorses that saved a tremendous amount of manual labor, but they were not that useful for decision support or knowledge management applications. The applications were developed and the data maintained in proprietary, vendor-dependent formats. The tools for creating reports that would appeal to managers as aids to decision making required considerable programming skill to use. A manager who wanted a particular report would need to define the requirements specifically and then wait weeks or months for a programmer to develop the code. Often the manager would not know enough about the underlying data or the way they were represented to make the requirements clear or even to realize that certain reports would be possible. Also, the systems themselves were often built or purchased to accommodate the needs of specific departments, which led to redundancy and incompatibilities. The result, after the long wait, may have been less than satisfying. Although gold existed in these systems, getting to it and turning it into useful knowledge could be a painful process involving many versions and revisions.

When microcomputers arrived at colleges and universities in large numbers, the centralized system architecture began evolving into a distributed model. The desktop computer could be used as a dumb terminal to access the applications running on the mainframe, but it had its own computing power and software. Partly because centralized technical staffs could not accommodate all the service requests, people developed their own applications on their desktops. These were often innovative systems built with spreadsheets or personal database programs that solved individual or departmental problems, but one result of this early mixing of centralized and distributed architectures was the evolution of the shadow system. Staff, or graduate assistants, would develop applications that stored data similar to what the centralized system held, but that were much more accessible for analysis, ad hoc queries, and modifications. Many of these turned into mission-critical systems containing valuable data. Because they were built separately, with a variety of software development tools, they were not integrated. The data were stored in different formats, and the content became inconsistent with what was in the mainframe. In some cases, data might be stored several times in different ways. An alumna's address, for example, might have appeared differently in databases maintained by her major department, the development office, and the alumni office, all in incompatible formats.

Many of these early desktop applications lacked the technical support and documentation common to centralized systems. When the person who built and maintained an important departmental application graduated or took another job, the application was abandoned or turned over to the centralized information technology (IT) department. The IT group was often ill equipped and reluctant to support it because the application may have been poorly designed, undocumented, or developed in tools not standard in their department. Those user-friendly database systems and spreadsheet applications were a welcome addition to the desktop for decision support, but they carried hidden costs that eventually surfaced.

The client-server architecture emerged as different types of computers were linked through networks. This approach is essentially a blend of the centralized host-based model and the distributed model. The clients are the fully capable computer processors on desktops, and the servers are hosts that can deliver data, applications, or other services to the clients. Servers can be large institutional mainframes, but they can also be minicomputers or high-end microcomputers. The number of servers at most institutions has grown quickly.

A goal of the client-server architectural approach was to tap the best characteristics of the earlier models and optimize unused power inside the microcomputers for real-time data. However, many client-server implementations have not delivered on their original promise, especially regarding the ability to deliver sophisticated decision support tools in an enterprisewide on-line environment. One reason is the sheer complexity of seamlessly integrating what has become a hodgepodge of servers, clients, mainframe applications, and stand-alone systems at many institutions. Migrating to an enterprisewide transactional system to serve various requirements is also a difficult task for organizations in which departments are accustomed to autonomous control. Another important factor is that transactional systems designed to track volumes of records are not generally well suited to the decision support and knowledge management applications that managers now expect.

The most recent architectural approach is a *netcentric* model in which the network, relying on rapidly evolving Internet standards, is the key player. Learning from the phenomenal success of the Internet, in which a wide variety of applications that adhere to common standards can be widely deployed over global networks, organizations are moving their enterprise architectures in the same direction. This approach will minimize the complexity at the desktop that generates so many costly help desk calls. Some organizations are already moving toward the next-generation terminal, which has considerable processing and computing power but no hard disk or local storage. The netcentric approach also offers many opportunities to extend access to a variety of information appliances, including small wireless devices such as personal digital assistants and cell phones.

Traditional separations between academic computing, administrative computing, and telecommunications have also affected the information architecture's evolution in academic institutions. These factors evolved independently, often with different infrastructures, reporting lines, and strategic approaches. More recently, many institutions have begun merging these functions into a single unit that reports to a chief information officer in an effort to improve integration. However, such massive changes take time.

For all of these reasons, many institutions have a mix of architectures and are only beginning to plan their information architecture strategically and systematically. Even institutions that purchased packaged software find shadow systems, academic applications for distance education, library catalogues, and other systems emerging that accommodate needs that those core applications do not meet. The result is a set of hills in which voluminous data are not well integrated or easily accessible.

The data in those hills are also not well understood as a whole landscape. Although individuals might be familiar with one area or another, no one really sees the big picture, so the knowledge needed to perform the integration may not exist. Routine questions involving a narrow domain may be relatively easy to answer, but unusual questions that require data integration from several areas can be a real challenge. For example, a provost may ask what appears to be a simple question: "How does library use vary among students with different majors?" It may be quite difficult to get an answer because the data needed are dispersed across several incompatible databases and systems and are coded differently. On the surface, it may seem a simple matter to assemble the masses of digitized data and create knowledge. In practice, the mixture of information architectures and databases that exists on most campuses can make the technical side of knowledge management quite challenging.

Turning Data into Knowledge: Decision Support Approaches

Although the underlying information architecture may be less than perfect, efforts to access information for decision support have been innovative and determined (Anand, 1998; Cios, 1998; Dhar and Stein, 1997a, 1997b; Turban and Aronson, 1997). Various approaches have emerged, and some of the best recognize that interactive decision support works best. Most people cannot clearly specify to a programmer exactly what they want and how they want it displayed. Often they do better with an interactive approach that allows them to explore results from a variety of related queries and build an understanding of the subject. The answer to one question leads to another question, and another. The process of turning data into knowledge benefits from an interaction in which the manager can sift, sort, and analyze in ad hoc and creative ways. The older legacy systems were less than successful. The data were difficult to integrate and access, and the tools were not flexible or user friendly enough.

A popular strategy for achieving this kind of interactivity is downloading data subsets from the major transactional system and then using microcomputer tools such as spreadsheets, statistical programs, or charting software to analyze them. The downloaded information is a snapshot of a certain portion of the transactional system, and the manager can import the data into various decision support software environments. Although the snapshot is out of date the moment after it is taken, much high-level decision making does not require up-to-the-minute information.

Another approach is the executive information system, which usually runs in conjunction with a transactional system and provides access to live data. Such systems provide managers with considerable flexibility about how they view organizational data within the transactional system. Graphics, charts, and tables are available. They also allow users to "drill down" from high-level summary data to increasingly detailed data that underlie these summaries. These systems can look attractive and useful when demonstrated on a small database, but many of them bog down transactional systems too much for widespread use.

Numerous approaches to decision support have emerged in the last decade and are worth examining. Designers of these new systems sought to overcome the obstacles that surfaced. Two such obstacles are that most institutions have data stored in many places and in many formats, and that transactional systems can come to a screeching halt if too many executives ask too many questions of the live data during peak hours.

Data Warehouses and On-Line Analytical Processing

One important advance in decision support is data warehouse development (Forcht and Cochran, 1999). Data warehouses are large-scale data storage facilities. They play key roles as knowledge bases for many organizations because they can store many types of data from any number of sources, and their designs do not need to accommodate enterprise-specific operational requirements. Instead, they are built specifically for decision support and knowledge management.

A data warehouse does not need to bear the design burdens associated with transactional systems, with all the business rules and processes that must be addressed—a definite advantage. A data warehouse can contain all the information about student records, for example, but need not include the logic to enforce the rules associated with course prerequisites or course loads. Another advantage is that the analytical tools are not combined with the transactional system's database, which must be optimized for transaction processing and data collection. For example, the transactional system must be able to compute an individual student's tuition quickly during peak registration periods. The data warehouse can emphasize speedy response to queries instead of transactions. Because they are separate systems, whatever computer resources the warehouse and its analytical tools require will not draw from the institution's major operational system.

Designing and populating the data warehouse and developing ways to refresh the data are more complicated than downloading a snapshot to a PC spreadsheet. The data can be drawn from many sources, which means the information must be unloaded from the source, loaded into a staging area, and then converted to a standard format. The conversion process addresses inconsistencies among data sources. For example, one data source may store student identification numbers in one format under the variable name SID, while another may use a different format and a different variable name. The data must also be scrubbed, that is, cleaned to catch the many errors that typically reside in diverse transactional systems, such as missing values or inaccurate zip codes. The data warehouse must then be updated periodically to add new data to historical records.

The real value for decision support and knowledge management comes from combining the data warehouse with sophisticated online analytical processing (OLAP). OLAP tools use a multidimensional approach to represent data and are also designed to facilitate flexible and rapid access to aggregated data. This is quite different from a transaction processing system in which the detail matters more than the aggregate. Transaction processing systems certainly generate reports, but they tend to be more routine, less frequent, and less useful for finding new relationships and patterns in the data. For OLAP, the data are structured as a hypercube in which the inner cells are the granular data elements and the outer cells are aggregate values, such as totals or averages. This design makes it possible for managers to interactively slice and dice a lot of data from many sources very rapidly and also to focus on detail if they choose.

Genetic Algorithms and Neural Nets

While advances in data warehouses and OLAP tools have greatly improved the kind of data-driven decision support that relies on interactive knowledge discovery, other data mining tools have emerged that do more of the discovery work on their own. Two of them were modeled after biological processes: genetic algorithms, based on the metaphor of natural selection, and neural nets, which draw principles from the human nervous system.

Genetic algorithms are optimization programs that help find good solutions to problems without the user's having to know much about how the problem is actually solved. Instead, the user identifies a "fitness function" that represents the qualifications for a good solution. The program begins with some random guesses about solutions and selects those that best match the fitness criteria in that generation. With each succeeding generation, the elements of those that matched best are combined and refined—much like the chromosomes in biological evolution—and the resulting solutions are again tested against the fitness benchmark. After several generations, the fitter solutions remain, while the less fit are eliminated. These algorithms have been applied successfully to problems in which it is difficult to describe the path to a good solution, but when users would know one when they saw it. Much of the work in developing a genetic algorithm approach involves defining the fitness function.

The neural net approach is inspired by how the brain's neurons find relationships and solve problems involving large amounts of data. The neuron receives information from the external environment and then transmits information to its neighbors across the synapse, or gap, between them by releasing chemicals called neurotransmitters. The main components of the neural network are neurodes, which model the neurons themselves, and weighted connections, which are analogous to synapses. Data are fed into an input layer of neurodes and then passed along to the intermediate layers. The strength of the connections between neurodes on different layers is adjusted to ensure that information from different sources is weighted appropriately to achieve the correct final result—at the output layer of neurodes. Using historical data, the neural network is trained so it keeps adjusting and readjusting the weighted connections that feed the intermediate layers until the model predicts the outcome at the output layer as accurately as possible. Then, after this learning period, the trained neural network can be used to solve new problems.

Both of these techniques use algorithms to identify patterns and relationships in immense quantities of data, but sometimes people do not easily understand the patterns they find. For example, they may identify some clusters of individuals who tend to act in certain ways based on the data, but characterizing or explaining those clusters may be difficult using ordinary human language.

Expert Systems

The expert system, another approach to technology in knowledge management programs, relies less on immense quantities of structured and digitized data and more on the knowledge that people in the organization already have but that has not been captured systematically. This gold can sometimes be even more difficult to strike since it is unstructured and resides in brain cells, e-mail, meeting minutes, filing cabinets, Web sites, and other locations. Software programs that model the decision-making processes of human experts have been developed for many different problem areas, including medicine, banking, and engineering. One of the first expert system programs was MYCIN, developed at Stanford University in the 1970s, which could diagnose blood infections based on if-then logic with certainty factors associated with each (Shortliffe, 1976).

Expert systems have become relatively widespread, and many innovations that improve accuracy and usability have been added since the early versions. They are essentially rule-based systems that tap human experts to systematize and document the processes—and rules—they use to solve problems. One example might be an expert system designed to evaluate a student's portfolio of transfer credits and then map them against course requirements in the new program. To develop such a system, the designers work closely with the academic adviser experts who know the enormously complex rules surrounding the transfer process.

A simple expert system would consist of a rule base, the working memory, and the rule interpreter. The rule base, not surprisingly, contains the rules derived from working with the experts on the problem domain. The working memory stores initial data, hypotheses, and intermediate conclusions. The rule interpreter matches data patterns against the rules using the working memory contents and then refreshes memory with new information based on the results. The expert system differs from a decision tree because there is some flexibility in how and when any particular rule is applied to the data. The entire system is more modular and flexible than a large decision tree, which moves from branch to branch in sequential steps.

The expert system can be fruitfully applied to situations where experts are available to explain their knowledge about how they make decisions in specific situations to the developer. The system works best with simpler problems so that building the model and rule base does not involve many subtle interactions among variables. Thus, the expert system is a decision support tool that works well in the exact opposite situations from genetic algorithms and neural networks.

Staking a Claim

Although knowledge management is not just about technology, any knowledge management program can go considerably further with the right technology and appropriate tools. It is frustrating to know that the information is out there but requires a great deal of work to access. We stress again the need for a strategic approach to planning and developing information architectures for the future so that university leaders can take full advantage of their data and properly manage their information assets.

Fortunately, technological innovations for knowledge discovery have advanced considerably. Systems have also become more accommodating to the nature of the data and its sources based on information architectures. We have described various strategies for finding relationships in data based on the manager's hypotheses and others that may work when the manager has no preconceived notions about what nuggets of information may be buried in those hills. A data warehouse is a critical element in most of these initiatives. If decision support and knowledge discovery are important in an organization, a warehouse is a worthwhile investment.

These examples of modern decision support and knowledge discovery tools cover only a portion of the landscape. Many other tools are emerging that consider how human beings process knowledge and make decisions, and they also recognize the realities that affect knowledge management technology. Fuzzy logic, for example, addresses the ambiguities in quantifying linguistic categories such as high and low or early and late. The dashboard, an intriguing example of a technological approach to knowledge management that is an updated analogue to the automobile's speedometer and odometer, is intended to provide information based on the manager's notion of a few critical success factors. The chief financial officer, for example, might want to have a window on the desktop PC that shows daily updates of revenues and expenses as well as year-to-date comparisons with last year's figures. The dashboard approach realizes that information overload is a major problem for any executive and emphasizes filtered and customized displays that provide real-time updates on only the most significant events.

The power of technology for data mining and knowledge discovery is enormous, and college and university leaders should also be aware of the dangers associated with the data collected on their campuses, especially about their students, faculty, staff, and alumni. Although legislation or policy protects some information, such as student academic records, much is not protected because it was never available before. Few campuses, for example, have a policy about student Internet-surfing data confidentiality as they do for student library use. The enormous quantity of data available on a valuable set of customers has created some dilemmas for university leaders. For example, a heated debate has arisen recently in higher education because some private companies, attracted by the chance to target advertising to upscale college students, have begun offering free Web design and customized portal services to colleges and universities. On the national scene, debate is focused on customer profiling and the danger these activities pose to individual privacy.

There is a lot of gold out there and the technology that is available to extract it in the form of knowledge is becoming more sophisticated. We have technological obstacles, organizational barriers, and ethical issues to confront, but knowledge, and its management, are what higher education is all about.

References

Anand, S. S. *Decision Support Using Data Mining*. London: Financial Times Management, 1998.

Cabena, P., and others. *Discovering Data Mining: From Concept to Implementation*. Englewood Cliffs, N.J.: Prentice Hall, 1998.

Cios, K. J. *Data Mining Methods for Knowledge Discovery*. Norwell, Mass.: Kluwer, 1998.

Cook, M. A. *Building Enterprise Information Architectures: Reengineering Information Systems*. Englewood Cliffs, N.J.: Prentice Hall, 1996.

Dhar, V., and Stein, R. *Intelligent Decision Support Methods: The Science of Knowledge Work*. Englewood Cliffs, N.J.: Prentice Hall, 1997a.

Dhar, V., and Stein, R. *Seven Methods for Transforming Corporate Data into Business Intelligence*. Englewood Cliffs, N.J.: Prentice Hall, 1997b.

Forcht, K. A., and Cochran, K. "Using Data Mining and Data Warehousing Techniques." *Industrial Management and Data Systems*, 1999, 5, 189–196.

O'Dell, C., and Grayson, C. J., Jr. "If Only We Knew What We Know: Identification and Transfer of Internal Best Practices." *California Management Review*, 1998, 40(3), 154–174.

Shortliffe, E. H. *Computer-Based Medical Consultations: MYCIN*. New York: Elsevier, 1976.

Turban, E., and Aronson, J. E. *Decision Support Systems and Intelligent Systems*. Englewood Cliffs, N.J.: Prentice Hall, 1997.

5

Revaluing Records

From Risk Management to Enterprise Management

Anne J. Gilliland-Swetland

Knowledge management offers a strategic systems approach to managing complex organizations. It is rooted in self-knowledge, which is both predictive and explanatory. A systems approach in this context refers to establishing a framework that makes it possible to discern complex interactions and patterns among an organization's disparate aspects. This, in turn, enables strategic planning and avoids short-term reactions to immediate concerns (Senge, 1990). Effective knowledge management requires all tangible organizational knowledge assets—among them, information, knowledge-based products, and organizational records—to be identifiable, reliable, authentic, persistent, and flexible. To meet these requirements, knowledge management must encompass not only the organization's agents, technologies, activities, processes, external and internal requirements and practices, products, and by-products, but also their complex interactions.

In this chapter I examine the evolving nature and scope of one kind of knowledge asset, organizational records, and discuss where record keeping and records management fit into the context of university knowledge management. Increased emphasis on record keeping in both administrative and academic activities, as well as a deeper construction of the organizational record, are necessary if systemwide knowledge management is to be achieved at academic institutions.

University Knowledge Management Context

Higher education institutions increasingly are reexamining their organizational systems, structures, and strategies and assessing ways to combine information technology with knowledge production to reinvent the university as a knowledge-based enterprise. Such an endeavor necessitates a clear understanding of an academic institution's business and institutionwide support for this underlying vision. This understanding is surprisingly difficult to attain and therefore to apply strategically, because universities fulfill many intangible functions and there are often competing perspectives about what their core business is.

Helen Samuels (1992), former archivist at the Massachusetts Institute of Technology, examined the modern university's complex nature and identified seven functions fundamental to its societal role and academic and administrative activities: conferring credentials, conveying knowledge, fostering socialization, conducting research, sustaining the institution, providing public service, and promoting culture. Academic institutions maintain both a knowledge production and administrative support infrastructure to carry out these functions. The knowledge production infrastructure supports teaching and research through activities such as library services, academic computing, and university publishing. The administrative support infrastructure sustains the institution and includes human resources, fiscal management, physical plant maintenance, and administrative record-keeping activities. Other functions, such as conferring credentials, providing public service, fostering socialization, and promoting culture, are arguably distributed in various ways across both infrastructures.

Ironically, the diverse structures and conventions that have evolved around supporting these functions in universities pose challenges for applying a systems approach to organizational knowledge management. Describing universities as "organized anarchies" (Cohen and March, 1986; Cohen, March, and Olsen, 1972) reflects dual hierarchies (academic and administrative) and the various fiefdoms thereunder, all with diverse and often disparate goals. There is inevitable tension within the institution regarding the knowledge-based enterprise metaphor. On one hand are administrators who manage the institution and develop its public profile and role in a rapidly changing social and technological environment. On the other are academics whose views are shaped by the beliefs and practices of their individual disciplines and the intellectual role that the university represents within society.

Characteristics and Requirements of Records

In the course of doing business, academic institutions create and manage records and supporting documents that have legal, fiscal, administrative, research, or historical significance. These records and associated materials by definition represent many of the complexities and interrelationships at work within academic institutions and are essential elements of institutional knowledge. Records in the strict legal sense are created for two purposes: to put an act into effect (with a contract, for example) or to serve as evidence or proof of an act that has been completed (for example, academic transcripts and receipts) (Duranti, 1998). These types of records are most frequently associated with administrative activities. Increasingly, however, and particularly as a result of research and teaching activities, records are being created that either support the official record but are not themselves legally required or provide narrative evidence of university activities but do not directly support the official record. In both instances, people are creating records with few controls. It is also important to remember that the university has many crucial, but less tangible, functions that include conveying knowledge, socializing, and promoting culture. These functions do not create many official records. Activities associated with these functions are not reflected in the official record, either because records are not mandated or because it meets the organization's needs not to keep detailed records of particular activities (Ngin, 1994; Gilliland-Swetland, 1996). Recognizing and redressing this situation is another important component of institutional knowledge management.

The Nature of Records

Several characteristics distinguish records from other kinds of organizational information and data. These characteristics are directly related to the way records can, and are, expected to show how an organization carries out its business and makes decisions.

Records are required for accountability purposes by law or by other regulatory or accreditation agencies. This may seem obvious, but it is important to acknowledge these requirements so they can be integrated within a knowledge management framework. Moreover, specific record-keeping practices may also be mandated. Even if they are not, these records may be subject to scrutiny if the organization is ever sued or audited.

Generating a record is an integral part of business and research. There is therefore an organic relationship between business processes and research activities and the records that are by-products of those processes and activities. Some records are created at the same time as the action that they document in order to put that action into effect, such as research contracts. Alternately, some are created subsequent to a business or research activity to prove that the activity occurred or to document completion. Two examples of this type of record are issuing a transcript to a student and creating an interim or final report to a granting agency. In either case, records are trusted as reliable sources when their integral relationship with the activity can be documented and verified.

Records are socially constructed entities; from a knowledge management perspective, understanding the procedural and documentary con-

texts may be just as important as record content. The physical and intellectual form of records reflects the functions they perform and the ways in which business is conducted. The physical form of records has changed greatly through the ages, from stone and clay tablets to papyrus and paper, and eventually to networked digital media. The intellectual form of records and their essential elements, however, appear to have changed considerably less because a record's function within an organization or society has remained more or less constant. Correspondence, for example, whether paper or electronic, typically still contains a cluster of elements indicating dates, places, people, and subjects associated with the correspondence; the text body of the correspondence; and closing matter, including signatures, annotations, and attachments. Through a brief visual scan of common records, such as internal memoranda, invoices, or ledgers, one can quickly understand what function the records perform, if not a detailed understanding of what the records contain.

Records, through how they are authorized, processed, and routed, reflect the complex interactions that occur during the daily course of business. For example, a record may need to be annotated, signed, and cosigned to be valid. Multipart records may also be distributed to several departments, where a part of the record will be integrated into a different record-keeping system for a different purpose. By tracking and understanding such activity, administrators can understand even more about the organization, including workflow, information flow, and the various organizational checks and balances that ensure reliability in business processes.

Records accumulate and are most valuable when viewed longitudinally and in the aggregate. By so doing, it is possible to discern patterns of organizational behavior and decision making, changes in processes, and trends in areas such as enrollment and sponsored research. Records also allow less tangible aspects of university life, such as the development of ideas, rhetoric, and political positions, to be traced.

Records have a natural redundancy that reflects record-creation and record-keeping practices. For example, a record may be completed as part of one business activity, and then copied to other business units, where they are annotated and filed. What may look like duplication, in that copies of the same information exist in multiple locations, in fact are different records because of their integration into different business and record-keeping contexts. Such redundancy has several important benefits, including the ability to check the integrity and completeness of a record, protection against accidental or deliberate loss of information, and access to information in many formats.

Creating Useful Records

A record's authority, trustworthiness, and authenticity is ultimately based on how its creation is controlled and how complete the record is. However, an organization must also be able to prove that such control was exercised (Duranti and MacNeil, 1997). Certain requirements for record keeping must therefore be met in order to ensure that records can effect their various purposes.

Records must be uniformly managed. Universities must have and follow uniform business procedures such as standard operating procedures (SOPs) and best practices to control the circumstances of record creation and disposition. These procedures might include data entry protocols, record registration and classification, and record retention scheduling. All procedures should be documented, and staff should be trained to implement the procedures. It should also be possible to prove that the resulting records were created according to these procedures.

Records must be useful. Sufficient descriptive information, or metadata, must be created to ensure that records can be easily identified, retrieved, and refiled, as well as put in their appropriate documentary context for as long as they are needed (Records Continuum Research Group, 1999).

Records must be auditable. Every time an active record is updated or otherwise altered, it should be possible to see its previous version, when it was changed, who changed it, and why.

Records must be immutable. When a record has been completed, it must be fixed so it cannot be deliberately or accidentally altered. Traditionally, completed records have been set aside at this point, that is, physically removed from where they were created and filed with other completed records.

Records must never be unmanaged. The chain of responsibility for and physical and intellectual custody of records must be documented and remain unbroken.

Records must selectively be preserved. Many records are strategically valuable to an organization long after they cease being active. Such records are generally scheduled for permanent or long-term retention and retained as archival records. To continue to serve as legal or historical evidence, these records must be preserved in such a way that it is possible to prove that all the above requirements have been and continue to be met.

The Evolving Nature and Scope of Organizational Records

As organizations implement digital information and communications systems to facilitate their daily activities, it has become increasingly difficult to establish whether these systems are capable of creating and managing records that meet the requirements set out for them. There is no doubt that many mission-critical areas within the university, such as accounting, student records, and personnel, use large-scale databases as efficient replacements for paper record-keeping systems and relate to these databases as if they were records. However, few if any of these areas have addressed the above-stated requirements as these digital systems were designed and maintained. Indeed, the reasons that most organizations have implemented information technology—to ensure that information can be efficiently stored and retrieved and can be readily updated—run counter to requirements for records—that they be immutable, cumulative, and redundant. As a result, information technology systems may have the unintended consequence of losing or destroying institutional knowledge.

Contemporary business and research processes and their electronic by-products are also poorly understood. Yet they remain strategically critical for organizational risk management, knowledge management, and enterprise management purposes. Moreover, the integrity—that is, the reliability and authenticity—of records created and maintained in electronic form is at risk because of systems design, technological obsolescence, use, and preservation issues—for example:

• Collaborative and distributed systems often result in records of multiple provenance, yet it is often unclear who has responsibilities and rights with regard to their long-term preservation, access, and reproduction. For example, a centralized student information system might be used for different purposes by many offices on a campus, each of which would traditionally have maintained its own record-keeping system. Similarly, a large-scale faculty research project might have academic and private sector collaborators at multiple locations—possibly even different national, legal, and organizational jurisdictions—all using computer-supported collaborative work technology (CSCW).

• Many digital systems, such as e-mail and geographic information systems, contain a mixture of potential record and nonrecord material. It must be possible to distinguish between the two and manage records according to record-keeping requirements. This is difficult to do, however, especially with e-mail because many users view their e-mail as analogous to a telephone call—and therefore not as a record—and may also mix official and personal business in the same message.

- Data warehouses and networked document creation and distribution create multiple variant versions of electronic records and make it difficult to establish where the official record resides.

- Guaranteeing that a record can be and has been fixed is problematic. Record layouts are constantly being updated and are frequently retrospectively enforced on previously created records, thus making it difficult to recreate what a record would have looked like contemporaneous with the act that created it. Moreover, each time a record is migrated for use on new media, hardware, or software, perceptible and imperceptible changes in function, layout, rendering, and bitstreams can occur.

- In information structures such as databases, all of a record's elements may not physically reside together. They may be pulled together virtually with a specialized view or database report. In addition, many key elements in records are inferred or implied from the record's procedural or documentary context rather than being explicitly stated. Both of these aspects make it hard to identify the physical entity that is the record and to manage it accordingly. It also leaves the records manager with a dilemma when it comes to how and when a record can be fixed and set aside. Should the records manager remove completed records from a system and transfer them to a records center or archive for preservation, or leave them in situ and find virtual ways of maintaining them that meet archival requirements?

- Establishing the authenticity of preserved records is also problematic, since rendering them software independent eliminates much of their evidential value, but leaving them in software-dependent form exposes them to perceptible and imperceptible changes. Digital signatures can prove some evidence that an active record is reliable, but they cannot ensure the authenticity of that record through time. The question here is on what basis the authenticity of preserved records can be established.

- Universities have not systematically addressed how to preserve the burgeoning quantities of electronic records that require long-term retention. Who has both the expertise and resources to manage records long term? Should universities collaborate on this activity, as they have done with book depositories? Could academic digital libraries take on this function because they will inevitably face some of the same problems preserving their digital assets?

On the positive side, more and more previously underdocumented aspects of university activity—such as the relationships between faculty and students, students and their peers, and collaborations among researchers—are leaving behind richly textured electronic traces in the form of e-mail, listserv archives, and Web pages. Although many of these traces carry sensitive ownership and privacy issues, they are providing tangible evidence of university functions for the first time. Such digital materials should therefore be factored into a wider concept of what is considered university records. More guidance should be provided to academics and students regarding how to manage them, not only as information, but also as records (Gilliland-Swetland and Kinney, 1994; Gilliland-Swetland, 1996).

Records as Organizational Knowledge Assets

The term *asset*, borrowed from the corporate world, suggests a new way of looking at knowledge. Knowledge assets are approached differently depending on whether they are addressed within an information management, risk management, knowledge management, or enterprise management framework. Knowledge assets can be tangible (for example, information, records, and products) or intangible (for example, individual expertise, collective memory, knowledge-related processes, and interactions). Organizational information assets include research data, library collections, and on-line information resources such as Web pages and listservs. In today's academic environments, on-line courseware, electronic publishing, digital libraries, and multimedia productions might all be considered, along with traditional research publications, textbooks, and research patents, as knowledge products.

A continuum exists between information, records, and knowledge products. Furthermore, there is an intricate and important interweaving of the intangible with the tangible (see Figure 5.1).

The boundaries between what is considered information, records, and knowledge products are fuzzy, and in fact each kind of asset can have components of the others in information-rich settings. Information management approaches are typically directed toward efficient, effective, and beneficial use of information assets and have included developing large-scale databases, indexing and cataloguing mechanisms for resource identification and discovery, collection development activities, and network management for wide access and interoperability. Information and records assets can be drawn together through knowledge management to form a more three-dimensional notion of the university. However, in doing so,

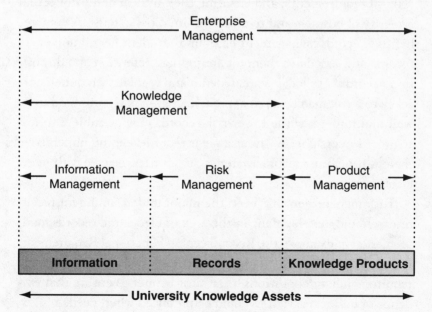

Figure 5.1. Managing University Knowledge Assets

the different objectives, practices, and requirements of each side must be recognized and factored in. There is also a fourth dimension that provides an even richer lens through which to look at the academic knowledge resource management: knowledge-based enterprise. This approach incorporates the knowledge management approach, but emphasizes the generation and exploitation of knowledge products generated by the university and its academic community. As Figure 5.1 indicates, therefore, three major rationales can be identified for managing records: risk management, knowledge management, and enterprise management.

Records, although they can provide an organization with a unique source of self-knowledge, have traditionally been undervalued as knowledge assets and are managed largely from a risk management perspective. Risk management generally ensures the accountability of the organization: determining the accuracy and propriety of financial transactions; monitoring the level of compliance with regulatory, funding agency, and university policy and procedural requirements; and ensuring the physical and intellectual integrity of business and research information systems. A comprehensive records management program that identifies all university records and schedules them for appropriate retention and disposition according to local, state, federal, and regulatory requirements is key to a risk management approach. High-risk records tend to be well maintained, while lower-risk records may be subject to less stringent oversight. Without a clear record-keeping imperative, there is little or no record awareness, as is often the case with many faculty activities.

Risk management has been the major underpinning for recent research and development in the area of electronic records management. For example, the Recordkeeping Functional Requirements Project at the University of Pittsburgh developed a set of functional requirements, or conditions, that must be met to ensure that evidence of business activities could be produced when needed (Cox, 1994). The project also developed a method for warranting record keeping derived from external authorities, such as statutes, regulations, standards, and professional guidelines, that is relevant to the individual organization. The organization can use this warrant to assess its degree of risk if it does not maintain its electronic records according to record-keeping requirements (Duff, 1998). This approach was effectively implemented in the Indiana University Electronic Records Management Project, where the university archives worked closely with university risk managers, including internal auditors and occupational safety professionals (Bantin, 1998, 1999).

Government agencies and records professionals also have been working to persuade organizations to manage their electronic records better by integrating functional requirements for electronic records management into record-keeping and quality-control standards. Two such standards are the U.S. Department of Defense's 5015.2 records management specification and the Australian AS 4390 records management standard, which are currently being proposed as standards within the ISO 9000 series of standards relating to quality control (Duff and McKemmish, forthcoming). Such a strategy increases risk for noncompliance within any organization subject to those standards.

Knowledge management provides a more positive incentive for organizational records management. Some of the processes involved include identifying, interrelating, making multiple versions of, and capturing information; making tacit knowledge explicit; and documenting the processes that create information. If a system is used as both an information system and a record-keeping system, and systems designers work to include the requirements of both, they can also maximize knowledge management. However, these systems are also the most complex to design and maintain because they must develop and manage value-added metadata and facilitate maximum content flexibility for multiple uses, audit trails, and long-term preservation.

Enterprise management reengineers business processes for strategic flexibility and potential revenue generation by creating knowledge capital. Such capital is manifest in a range of knowledge products. The ability to control the capital has been transformed by implementing networked communications and multimedia technology. Although universities and individual academics have become much more sophisticated about tracking intellectual property aspects such as copyright and patents, they have not invested the same care in establishing responsibility and identifying resources for proving that ownership. To do so requires sound record keeping by every part of the organization. Anyone undertaking an activity likely to yield such products should keep records to substantiate their intellectual claims.

Archives as a Function Rather Than a Place

University archives are changing just as records are evolving. Traditionally, active records have fallen under the purview of institutional records management programs, and inactive ones become the responsibility of the university archives. Once transferred to the archives, they are integrated with previous records generated by the same function, regardless of whether the records are electronic or paper. The university archive plays two important roles in organizational knowledge management. First, it is one of the few units within the university that maintains an organizationwide, nonaligned perspective on the university and its development over time. Second, it is an interface between the administrative and the research infrastructures of the university. Records created through the university's business and research processes are also valuable sources for researchers, including students, scholars, academic administrators, journalists, and architects.

In the past, the university archive has primarily been characterized as a place and the archivists as record custodians, but the issues raised by creating and preserving electronic records, as well as new research modes, are causing more people to see the archives as a function, not a place (Upward and McKemmish, 1994). Electronic records experts have argued for nearly two decades that archivists must be involved with records and record-keeping systems from the moment they are conceived, and they must work with systems designers and record creators to ensure the systems and their records meet record-keeping and long-term preservation requirements. Increasingly, archival functions are being integrated across the continuum of record creation, use, reuse, and preservation. By developing archival and record-keeping metadata schemes, universities can ensure that records meet both administrative and research use requirements throughout their life (Records Continuum Research Group, 1999). This goal is also being accomplished with "postcustodial" approaches, whereby inactive records remain in the system where they were created (meeting stringent requirements set by the university archives), but the archivists assume responsibility for intellectual access and record authenticity. Archivists have also been developing a deeper understanding of university functions (Bantin, 1999) and how they might be documented in new ways by such materials as course Web pages, student electronic conferences, and Web-based collaborative research sites (Gilliland-Swetland, 1995; Gilliland-Swetland and Kinney, 1994).

Conclusion

The evolving role, requirements, and nature of records and the university archives have been largely overlooked in the development of university knowledge management frameworks. With the impact of information and communications technology, it is critical to ensure that both electronic and traditional records are created and maintained in ways that maximize the knowledge and insight they can provide to the university and its members, while also ensuring that the university is not exposed to liability.

To satisfy both objectives, several strategic issues need to be addressed by institutional leaders. These issues center on raising record consciousness across the university, identifying and redressing gaps and weaknesses in documentation and record-keeping activities, and identifying the technological, fiscal, and human resources needed to ensure effective creation and preservation of trustworthy records. Addressing electronic record issues cannot wait. Without explicit and timely action, many will not survive beyond their immediate period of use. The capacity of those that do persist to play a useful role in organizational knowledge management will be diminished because their scope and integrity will have been compromised. While ultimately how each organization addresses these issues must be customized to its own situation, there are some overall strategies that can be applied:

- Explicitly identify and acknowledge the importance and role of records and record-keeping practices in terms of their contribution to organizational knowledge management.

- Appoint a team of stakeholders with representatives from areas of the university with a direct interest in organizational records (for example, university archives, university legal counsel, financial services, internal audit, student records, hospital records, sponsored research, information technology, university libraries) as well as teaching and research faculty. The team should develop functional requirements for the design and preservation of electronic record-keeping systems and promote sound record-keeping practices within members' respective areas.

- Identify and assign specific authority and responsibility for implementing functional requirements in the design of new and existing electronic records systems, as well as for developing metadata that will ensure maximum accessibility, compilation, and reversioning of records and the information they contain.

- Integrate programmatically inactive and archival records with current records. A major value of records for knowledge management purposes lies in longitudinal collectivity and referential integrity.

- Provide for long-term storage and preservation of software-dependent electronic records and other mission-critical university documentation, including that generated by researchers in the form of digital data and reciprocated links and references to resulting electronic and traditional publications. Because the resources and expertise required to develop a preservation program are likely to be extensive, but the electronic materials themselves do not require a specific physical location, one possible approach might be a consortium model such as has been used by some universities for off-site library storage, digital library development, or data archives.

- Assess record-keeping needs for academic research and enterprise and educate academic researchers about how best to address them.

References

Bantin, P. "Developing a Strategy for Managing Electronic Records—The Findings of the Indiana University Electronic Records Project." *American Archivist*, 1998, *61*, 328–364.

Bantin, P. "The Indiana University Electronic Records Project Revisited." *American Archivist*, 1999, *62*, 153–163.

Cohen, M. D., and March, J. G. *Leadership and Ambiguity: The American College President*. (2nd ed.) Cambridge, Mass.: Harvard Business School Press, 1986.

Cohen, M. D., March, J. G., and Olsen, J. P. "Garbage Can Model of Organizational Choice." *Administrative Science Quarterly*, 1972, *17*, 1–25.

Cox, R. J. "Re-Discovering the Archival Mission: The Recordkeeping Functional Requirements Project at the University of Pittsburgh, a Progress Report." *Archives and Museum Informatics*, 1994, *8*, 279–300.

Duff, W. "Harnessing the Power of Warrant." *American Archivist*, 1998, *61*, 88–105.

Duff, W., and McKemmish, S. "Metadata and ISO Compliance." *Information Management Journal*, forthcoming.

Duranti, L. *Diplomatics: New Uses for an Old Science*. Lanham, Md.: Society of American Archivists, Association of Canadian Archivists, and Scarecrow Press, 1998.

Duranti, L., and MacNeil, H. "The Preservation of the Integrity of Electronic Records: An Overview of the UBC-MAS Research Project." *Archivaria*, 1997, *42*, 46–67.

Gilliland-Swetland, A. J. "Digital Communications: Documentary Opportunities Not to Be Missed." *Archival Issues*, 1995, *20*(1), 39–50.

Gilliland-Swetland, A. J. *Policy and Politics: A Case Study in the Management of Electronic Communications at the University of Michigan*. Chicago: Society of American Archivists, 1996.

Gilliland-Swetland, A. J., and Kinney, G. T. "Uses of Electronic Communications to Document an Academic Community: A Research Report." *Archivaria*, 1994, *38*, 79–96.

Ngin, P. M. "Recordkeeping Practices of Nurses in Hospitals." *American Archivist*, 1994, *57*, 616–630.

Records Continuum Research Group, Monash University. "Recordkeeping Metadata." [www.sims.monash.edu.au/rcrg/research/spirt/index.html]. 1999.

Samuels, H. W. *Varsity Letters: Documenting Modern Colleges and Universities*. Metuchen, N.J.: Society of American Archivists and Scarecrow Press, 1992.

Senge, P. M. *The Fifth Discipline: The Art and Practice of the Learning Organization*. New York: Doubleday, 1990.

Upward, F., and McKemmish, S. "Somewhere Beyond Custody." *Archives and Manuscripts*, 1994, *22*, 136–149.

6

Case Study

Knowledge Management Alleviates the Computing Support Crisis at Indiana University

Brian D. Voss

Since the dawn of the personal computer age in the 1980s, the issue of how to support the widespread use of computing has been with us. As this desktop computing revolution gained momentum, supporting its use in the enterprise quickly advanced from issue to concern, and eventually to crisis.

The information technology support crisis in higher education (McClure, Smith, and Sitko, 1997) is really a knowledge problem that can be addressed through knowledge management and knowledge transfer. At its core is an environment in which many people are required to make productive use of information technology, but the knowledge of how to do that is in the heads of a relatively few experts. The challenge that colleges and universities are facing is how to do a better job of managing and distributing the knowledge about information technology that exists in these institutions to ensure that users will be able to leverage the power of information technology (IT).

To address this challenge at Indiana University (IU), we have developed what we call the leveraged support model (LSM), a knowledge management application that has two key components: the Indiana University Knowledge Base and a comprehensive user education (knowledge transfer) approach.

The model is a solution to an institutional knowledge problem in that it seeks to organize the flow of expert knowledge, ensuring that it is where it is needed when it is needed. Its objective is to allow the institution to continue to develop its information technology environment without a corequisite growth in resources devoted to supporting that environment.

This chapter describes this model, with a focus on the Knowledge Base—how it evolved, what it does, how it is maintained, and its benefits—and the education of users that has enabled them to support themselves in the use of IT in their work.

Leveraged Support Model

In today's IT support environments, several support models have emerged (McClure, Smith, and Lockard, 1999). The classic set includes:

- *Centralized*. The preponderance of support is based in resources in a centrally located organization, and service is delivered directly to end users.

- *Decentralized*. Resources are divided among subunits of the enterprise to deliver support to end users.

- *Haphazard*. This model results if no one in the enterprise exercises leadership by addressing user expectations and satisfaction.

- *Distributed*. Both centralized and subunit-based resources blend in some fashion to meet the support needs of the enterprise.

Indiana University has elected to pursue the distributed model, which has three basic components:

- Support provided by the central IT organization

- Support provided by staff who reside in departments

- Support provided by the users of IT themselves (Voss, 1998)

The success of this model depends on how well the central IT organization assumes responsibility for ensuring the other two components of support. The most important component is the third, self-support, because there are more users than there are central and departmental support providers put together.

To tap the potential of the model, the vast majority of support must be provided through user self-support mechanisms. Users must be well educated and trained so that they can deal with most of the support issues that arise during their interaction with the technology. However, although IT is a critical part of nearly everyone's work today, it is not feasible to expect users to become IT professionals. So once we have imparted as much IT training as they can absorb, we then must augment that training with easy-to-use support tools that allow users to support their own technology needs.

One of the most effective of such self-support tools is IU's Knowledge Base, a collection of the knowledge needed by any campus constituent engaged in addressing the support of IT use. This collection is made available electronically, for automated on-line retrieval by those with a need for the information. Think of it as a collection of problems and their associated solutions, stored in a database and retrieved on demand by anyone who can identify a problem to the system and interpret the resolution the system provides.

Evolution of the Indiana University Knowledge Base

Even at Indiana University, where the IT support challenge has received much attention for nearly twelve years, no one predicted the current set of tools and outcomes at the outset. Rather, we reacted to a prevailing set of conditions and chose paths that not only addressed those conditions but set us on a road to later success.

What Was the Problem?

With constrained support resources and rapid turnover in the entry-level positions that were typical of the central IT organizations, these organizations had increasing difficulty retaining the expert knowledge that developed in the staff who provided the support. Initially, then, the challenge was for the central organization to retain its intellectual capital, since it did not have the resources (or organizational power) to retain the individuals themselves. With the rapid turnover of staff, the problem was how to continue to give adequate support to all users with questions, with a constant need to bring in new (and relatively unskilled) labor. Nonappointed student staff—a staff that turned over every year—primarily delivered support beginning in the late 1980s. How could the central IT organization retain the knowledge developed in these individuals for periods longer than their brief stays with the organization, and how could that knowledge be leveraged by new consultants?

People who were hired were given an assessment of their skill level and then were put through a customized course of basic training. Not much time was available for this training, because new staff arrived at the help desk usually about a week before the crunch of support need. And like all other forms of fast training, it left these individuals less than equipped to deal with the barrage of questions they would receive during their first active week on the telephones.

Response to the Problem: The Internal Knowledge Base

Faced with this challenge, the central support organization found a creative solution. A database of support information was built, taking the form of frequently asked questions (FAQs) and the answers to those questions, crafted by skilled staff who quickly moved on with their careers. The knowledge built by these generations of help desk staff was retained and used by new staff as a tool as they built the skills needed to address the problems presented in the flood of telephone calls from users.

If a problem came in to an individual who did not know how to solve it, that person asked the caller to hold for a moment while he or she used the FAQ to look up the answer. In the process of providing a solution to the callers, the support providers also learned something new themselves. Thus, they enriched their own skill—and the skill level of the central support function—using the knowledge of their "ancestors." The Indiana University Knowledge Base was born!

As time passed, the number of entries into this set of FAQs grew to the point where callers did not possess the patience required to give the support provider time to page through hundreds of problems and solutions. As well, some of the problems and solutions in the Knowledge Base were no longer valid, having been eliminated by advances in technology in hardware and software, or changed by these same factors. So two challenges emerged: (1) a need to search quickly through a growing database of problems and solutions and (2) a need to ensure that the information was accurate based on the changes to the environment over time.

The central support organization began to apportion a small but growing share of its resources to the development of a means to search the Knowledge Base quickly and to ensure that the information in it was fresh, accurate, and useful. Advances in database management systems made it possible to accomplish the former. Periodic meetings of the "knowledge trust" to review, edit, and improve the information in the Knowledge Base accomplished the latter. As these two initiatives advanced in parallel, the Knowledge Base grew to a valued, almost indispensable resource for the support function. And for many years through the early and mid-1990s, it was the fundamental reason that the IT organization was able to address the support needs of the community of users.

The Internal Knowledge Base Moves Out into the Community

The distributed support model was advancing as more and more departments had their own local support providers (LSPs) who were called on to support their constituent users, closer to home. These staff too had a need to leverage the knowledge available through-out the institution.

Access to the Knowledge Base became decentralized, first to the LSPs and then to the users, in response to demand by these con-stituencies for more effective means of obtaining needed knowledge. This process of release of the Knowledge Base occurred over two to three years as this tool found its way from the help desk to the broader community through a process of give and take. Initially this was not the result of a plan to decentralize the tool but was prompted by a conversation between a help desk staff member and an LSP who asked if he could use the Knowledge Base system to support users in his department.

Help desk staff did not think the internal Knowledge Base would work well in the external community, even when wielded by tal-ented LSP staff. But the value of the idea was sufficient to justify the effort to polish the tool to make it more usable by these exter-nal, departmental technical staff. More effort went into the search engine as well as the process of ensuring the quality of the infor-mation held in the Knowledge Base. This was now a tool going pub-lic. The Knowledge Base would have to be solid, or else it would fail in the furnace of LSP use; as well, it would be a setback to the advances taking place in the development of the relationship with the LSP community.

All of this attention and effort was rewarded when the Knowl-edge Base was distributed and accepted by the LSP community. A community of hundreds of internal IT organization and external LSP staff was now becoming dependent on this tool. It did not take long before a user observing an LSP access the Knowledge Base sug-gested the value of making it available directly to users.

If the Knowledge Base was to be successfully deployed beyond several hundred skilled support providers to the masses of end users, it would need an easy-to-use interface. At about this time, the World Wide Web was emerging as a new technology tool, and it became clear that it would provide the interface needed for IU's

Knowledge Base. This Web-based interface would improve all aspects of the Knowledge Base's use by the entire community—central support staff, LSPs, and end users.

Again, as use of the Knowledge Base spread, its value and the IT organization's reputation depended even more heavily on its ease of use, performance, and the accuracy of the information within it. By now, the Knowledge Base had become a core responsibility set for a portion of the central support organization. The move to broaden its use to the community at large would mean that it would ascend to a position of primary concern to the IT organization. And as it was more broadly used, the skill of all the contributors would be leveraged across the institution.

Support provider staff would come and go, especially as the end of the 1990s resulted in a highly mobile IT support staff. But the Knowledge Base would be there, holding the best of the past and continually updated with the most current information available.

How Does the Knowledge Base Help Us with Knowledge Management Today?

If we expect users to provide a very large share of their own support service, how do we position them to do that? Today the problem being addressed is not a lack of information to support the use of IT. On the contrary, there is an abundance of information available—too much, in fact. The problem is how to get through that 100-foot haystack of information to find the particular needle needed to solve a particular user's current problem.

How Is the Knowledge Base Delivered to Users?

The Knowledge Base is essentially an expert system for using information technology. The interface is via the most pervasive application available: the Web. The user enters the question (keywords and even "plain English" questions), and the system searches an information database for possible answers to the question. Those answers are then offered to the user, who can then resolve the problem.

The Knowledge Base is a system with three physical components:

- A repository of problems and their resolutions (currently holding over six thousand entries)

- A search engine to sort through that repository (currently handling over fifty thousand queries each week)

- A user interface that allows a user to engage the search engine to manage the data currently used by hundreds of thousands of users worldwide

By comparison, Indiana University's other means of IT support—telephone, e-mail, and walk-in—are capable of answering only about seven thousand questions each month.

However, the Knowledge Base is more than just these physical components. It is an electronic and physical manifestation of the knowledge of the people who built it and maintain it.

How Is the Knowledge Base Maintained?

An unforeseen outcome was that the Knowledge Base has become the collective memory of all parties involved in IT support—even those no longer with the IT organization. It has an expert system quality to it. As well, with the development of a Knowledge Base–entry interface, all support staff can submit entries based on the questions they are handling through the more traditional forms of support interaction. And users themselves can submit questions and answers to the Knowledge Base, thus extending broadly the base of knowledge held.

Within the support center is a Knowledge Base team composed of an appointed team leader, seven appointed professional staff, and approximately four full-time-equivalent staff of nonappointed student hourly help tasked with the ongoing maintenance of the knowledge in the Knowledge Base. In years past, the process of refreshing the Knowledge Base occurred at the start of each semester, which soon became a task done twice a semester. Now the Knowledge Base is refreshed daily, with major content reviews quarterly.

What Has Been the Outcome?

The Knowledge Base has become the primary resource for providing support for the use of information technology at Indiana University. It also has been expanded to deal with a variety of other support needs. Domains have been established for departments and other service providers, so that they can provide not-necessarily-technical information to their specific constituencies. This proved particularly useful in the implementation of several enterprisewide information systems.

One such example was IU's financial information system. The department sponsoring that application, the Financial Management Services, used a Knowledge Base domain to make available knowledge about the function of the application, as well as information regarding various financial processes in place in the institution. It was easy for this office to use the Knowledge Base to collect knowledge about the system and their services and to have a ready means of making that knowledge available to their customers.

The presence and importance of the Knowledge Base to the university support environment also has provided a framework for the overall support function. Ultimately every support interaction can benefit users beyond those simply involved in a one-to-one support situation. So we have developed a process by which all support interactions are considered as knowledge entries of the Knowledge Base. Through the development of a "workbench" application, front-line support staff are able to enter problems and resolutions into the Knowledge Base review process. In cases where these front-line resources need to pass the problem (due to complexity) to a second or third tier of support, those who may resolve the problem at each step are encouraged to determine if the Knowledge Base should be updated to reflect the outcome of any particular problem resolution event. This focus on the Knowledge Base has guided us to be more structured in our general support function, and we believe it has made our traditional forms of interaction better, as well as allowing them to serve the whole community of users.

Why Has the Knowledge Base Been So Successful?

What makes the Knowledge Base work and gives it value is not the technology, which is based on fairly pedestrian components: flat files, search engines, and a Web interface. Rather, its success stems from the people behind it. The Knowledge Base is like a small child; it demands constant attention to prevent it from running amok. Today we can spread misinformation with lightning speed, so it is critical that we constantly review and renew the knowledge based in this important tool.

The Knowledge Base has been successful largely because it became a matter of pride to the central support organization that it be successful. In human terms, we all want to be admired for our intelligence and recognized for the knowledge we have to bring to bear in solving problems. That need is behind the success of the Knowledge Base. It very much represents the mind and skill of the people who built it and maintain it.

Like any other good product, it sells itself. We judge the Knowledge Base by the number of hits it receives each week (over fifty thousand at last count), the leveling off of calls to our support center, the satisfaction users display when surveyed about the effectiveness of the Knowledge Base, and even the national recognition it has received as a leading support resource on the Internet.

The Second Component: Knowledge Transfer

The Knowledge Base is a tool that end users can use to leverage the skill of others and apply it to their own support needs. But in the leveraged support model, a tool is only part of the solution. We must find a way for IT users to develop a basic level of skill so that they can effectively make use of the institution's investment in IT infrastructure.

The better educated and trained users are, the better prepared they will be to support themselves. In the past, many chief information officers viewed user education as an auxiliary enterprise. Essentially, education was the user's responsibility, and although the IT organization might provide it, it was not part of its base function and hence was placed on a cost recovery basis. This was a flaw in many central IT structures during the IT support crisis, and in fact probably contributed greatly to the crisis in the first place.

Fundamentally, the issue is that of knowledge transfer, from the IT organization to the user. And the IT organization needs to understand that its role in knowledge management includes ensuring that the users have the skills necessary to make use of the IT tools on their desktops.

Support is a function of all three levels of the leveraged support model. If LSPs or end users lack the knowledge and skill to provide their share of the support needed, then the natural tension of the environment will force this load back on the central IT organization. So education and training are very much a critical function for the IT organization to provide in fulfilling its role in the LSM. It is a responsibility that, if not provided out of a sense of altruism, should be provided out of an instinct for self-preservation. Institutions that have successfully addressed the IT support crisis have done so by recognizing the need for both support tools and education. If they do not have the former in an advanced form, then they compensate by improving on the latter.

For LSPs, this education takes the form of free (or highly subsidized) education programs that equip them with high-end technology support skills. Often these programs make use of vendor-sponsored training and certification offerings. But a key to success is that the IT organization takes ownership of ensuring that LSPs are indeed well trained and thus well enabled to handle their role in the LSM.

For end users, this education takes the form of free (or highly subsidized) education programs that equip them with the basic technology use skills they need to use IT effectively. The challenge of traditional, in-class instruction is most likely beyond the resources and capabilities of even the most dedicated and well-financed IT organization. However, the market has responded with a number of tools, especially computer-based training. This training is like the Knowledge Base: it uses technology and the desktop computer to allow users to train themselves. But the responsibility to ensure that the users have these new education tools, in addition to more traditional forms, rests squarely with the IT organization. The key to success is that the IT organization takes ownership for ensuring that users are well trained and thus well enabled to handle their role in the LSM.

Conclusion

Information technology is a part of today's higher education environment. What is not always recognized is that the costs of supporting the use of information technology are greatly more significant and long-standing than the costs of acquiring it. If the need for a strong and structured technology support environment is not acknowledged, an institution can waste its capital investment in technology, acquiring and placing hardware and software that is not used effectively (if at all). And if this need is not addressed properly, the institution can get caught in a spending spiral for technology support that exceeds the spending spiral for technology itself.

Key factors for successful IT knowledge management include the following:

- *Organizing effectively to deliver support.* The central IT organization organizes its support function to maximize the benefit of a leveraged support model. Units or teams are put into place to focus on the key areas of education, local support provision, and end user support services, each focusing on a different target audience for knowledge transfer.

- *Providing local support.* The best support for IT users is that which is closest to them. Access to information is on their desktops; their local support provider is just down the hall. For users to make the best use of the centrally leveraged knowledge, they need skilled support providers on site who are well prepared to deal with specific local support needs.

- *Emphasizing knowledge transfer to local support providers.* The better trained and skilled that the local support providers are, the higher the quality of support they deliver to their constituents and the more the central IT organization benefits. The IT organization facilitates opportunities for local support providers to learn from experts as well as share knowledge with their colleagues in other departments.

- *Emphasizing knowledge transfer to users.* The better trained the users of IT are, the better able they are to fulfill their own roles in the institution. User education is a key to IT knowledge management, through instructor-led classes as well as computer-based training.

- *Providing tools that enable user self-support.* Whether using a specially developed tool such as the IU Knowledge Base or simply a collection of available commercial and Internet information resources, the institution ensures that users have the knowledge they need to use their own technology to support their needs.

- *Providing deep target areas of support knowledge.* When the topic is more complicated, the knowledge offered by the IT organization to local support providers and high-end users alike is deeper. The IT organization provides these deep target areas of IT support knowledge to establish the base for knowledge transfer. Examples of such areas are statistical and mathematical application support, electronic text support, and research computing support (Voss, Alspaugh, Kava, and Porter, 1998).

Throughout this chapter, we have seen how one university has made substantial progress in addressing what has been essentially a knowledge management problem: the support of the use of information technology. The leveraged support model and the Knowledge Base are knowledge management tools that help Indiana University leverage its scarce IT knowledge resources and ultimately allow campus IT users to support their own use of information technology.

We have made significant investments in the technology of support as well as in the technology infrastructure on the desktops, in the walls, in the ground beneath our campuses, and in our central machine rooms. In the end, however, improving how we manage IT knowledge has had as much to do with the people involved—how they are organized and their motivated approach toward use of knowledge in support of technology—than it has had to do with the technology infrastructure per se. We have had an almost single-minded approach to ensuring that support services were abundant, of high quality, and dedicated to transferring knowledge to those who need it, and this has made all the difference.

References

McClure, P. A., Smith, J. W., and Lockard, T. W. "Distributed Computing Support." In D. G. Oblinger and R. N. Katz (eds.), *Renewing Administration—Preparing Colleges and Universities for the 21st Century.* Bolton, Mass.: Anker, 1999.

McClure, P. A., Smith, J. W., and Sitko, T. D. *The Crisis in Information Technology Support: Has Our Current Model Reached Its Limit?* Boulder, Colo.: CAUSE, 1997. [http://www.educause.edu/ir/library/html/pub3016/16index.html].

Voss, B. D. "Indiana University Leveraged Support Model." Paper prepared for the Coalition for Networked Information's Institution Wide Information Strategies Project. [www.cni.org/projects/iwis/97rep/iwis97.indiana.html]. 1998.

Voss, B. D., Alspaugh, G. R., Kava, M. P., and Porter, T. M. "Supporting Departmentally Based IT Support Providers." Preconference workshop presented at the 1998 CAUSE Annual Conference, Seattle, Dec. 1998.

A Knowledge Management Action Agenda

Gerald Bernbom

The preceding chapters have presented a substantive overview of the field of knowledge management and offer a number of specific recommendations and relevant observations for leaders in colleges and universities. The chapter authors address a broad range of issues that are important for higher education: campus administration and organization, innovation and knowledge asset management, intellectual property, scholarly communication, information management, archives and records management, and information technology support.

In Chapter One, Jillinda Kidwell, Karen Vander Linde, and Sandra Johnson offer some specific advice to institutions that may want to undertake a knowledge management initiative:

- Begin with a strategy that defines the goal of the program.

- Build the organizational infrastructure—human resources, financial measurements of success, and information technology—to support the initiative.

- Keep information technology in a proper perspective, as an enabler of larger institutional goals.

- Establish criteria by which to measure the impact of knowledge management in objective terms: cost reductions, increased effectiveness, removal of barriers to innovation, and increased customer satisfaction.

- Select a pilot project to test out ideas, determine their usefulness, and build credibility for the initiative based on real accomplishments.

- Develop a detailed plan of action, and define resources, roles, and incentives.

- Assess the results of the pilot project and refine the plan of action based on measured results.

In Chapter Two, Blaise Cronin and Elisabeth Davenport present three perspectives on knowledge management, focusing on process and the discovery of latent value, access and the codification of content, and culture and the importance of interaction in knowledge creation and management:

- Regarding process engineering and latent value, they observe that colleges and universities may have any number of underperforming knowledge assets—patents, prototypes, courseware, specialized faculty expertise, and unique archival collections—whose value is considerable but untapped.

- Regarding access engineering, they make the important observation that universal schemes of knowledge organization often fall short of meeting the fast-changing needs of scholarship in emerging and evolving fields of study, which are often interdisciplinary, interinstitutional, and international in scope. This observation challenges traditional library practices of uniform classification and emphasizes the importance of organizing knowledge in ways that are flexible, customized, locally relevant, and often discipline-specific.

- The discussion of cultural engineering shifts the focus from knowledge to knowing and from content to inter-action, with the observation that successful institutions of higher education will use knowledge management to become more self-aware, reflective, and adaptive to their environment, with a culture distinguished by sharing and cooperation.

In Chapter Three, Peter Lyman examines knowledge manage-ment in higher education in four areas: (1) network infrastructure and knowledge management, (2) scholarly communication, (3) institutional boundaries and the influences of e-commerce, and (4) the issues of intellectual property and innovation. In the process he raises a number of important questions for higher edu-cation leaders to consider, among them the following:

- What is the impact of information technologies on the dif-ferent kinds of knowledge discovery within an institution?

- Why is higher education a leader in invention but slow to use the network to create innovative new modes of teaching and learning, research, and service?

- Where is organizational innovation in higher educa-tion? Is it a goal?

- How would higher education change if staff were defined as knowledge workers?

- What will be the impact of the intellectual property revolution on higher education?

- How can experimentation with new modes of scholarly communication be optimized for the needs of the vari-ous disciplines and professions?

- What business model will support scholarly publishing?

- What is the future of the knowledge management services provided by learned societies?

- What kind of quality control is applicable to collaborative work and network publication for tenure and promotion decisions?

- Who owns the rights to the processes and products of knowledge discovery?

- Does today's pedagogy and curriculum properly prepare students to work in a knowledge economy?

In Chapter Four, Patricia Wallace and Donald Riley survey the information technology landscape, examining several significant influences of information technology on decision support, knowledge discovery, and knowledge management. They offer a number of suggestions and recommendations, including the following:

- A strategic approach to developing an information architecture is needed so that campus leaders can take full advantage of the volumes of data that are collected and managed in their institution's information systems.

- A data warehouse is a critical element to provide complete, timely, and reliable information for decision support and knowledge discovery.

- The power of technology for data mining is enormous, with both positive and negative consequences. Higher education leaders should be aware of the dangers associated with data collected on their campuses, especially as they relate to the privacy of individual students, faculty, staff, and alumni.

- New applications of technology create new data that never before existed. Campus leaders should review policies regarding the confidentiality of data that keeps track of individual Internet use (much as current policies protect the confidentiality of individual library use).

In Chapter Five, Anne Gilliland-Swetland provides an urgently needed discussion of key issues involved in managing the vital records of colleges and universities, especially records that increasingly are being stored in digital form. Without explicit and timely action, many of the records being created today will not survive. She thus recommends a number of concrete action steps for campus leaders:

- Explicitly acknowledge the importance and role of records and record-keeping practices to effective organizational management.

- Appoint a team of stakeholders to develop functional requirements for the design and preservation of electronic record-keeping systems and to promote sound record-keeping practices within their respective areas.

- Assign specific authority and responsibility for implementing functional requirements in the design of new and existing electronic records systems.

- Provide for long-term storage and preservation of software-dependent electronic records and other mission-critical university documentation, including that generated by researchers in the form of digital data.

- Assess record-keeping needs for academic research and educate academic researchers about how best to address these requirements.

Finally, in Chapter Six, Brian Voss presents a case study of a successful knowledge management application that makes use of an innovative organizational model for organizing and sharing institutional knowledge (the leveraged support model) as part of an overall information technology support service. He also describes the evolution of an effective application of computer technology (the Indiana University Knowledge Base) to the problem of collecting vital knowledge about answers to IT support problems, storing these answers and keeping them current, searching the repository in response to user inquiries, and delivering the right information when and where it is needed. Based on this case study, some key success factors for this knowledge management application include the following:

- *Organizing effectively to deliver support.* The central IT organization organizes its support function to focus on the key areas of education, local support provision, and end user support services, each emphasizing a different target audience for knowledge transfer.

- *Emphasizing knowledge transfer to local support providers.* The IT organization facilitates opportunities for local support providers to learn from experts as well as share knowledge with their colleagues in other departments.

- *Emphasizing knowledge transfer to users.* User education is a key to IT knowledge management, through instructor-led classes as well as computer-based training.

- *Providing tools that enable user self-support.* Whether it is a tool such as the IU Knowledge Base or simply a collection of commercial and Internet information resources, the institution ensures that users have the knowledge they need to use their own technology to support their needs.

- *Providing deep target areas of support knowledge.* When the topic is more complicated, the knowledge offered by the IT organization to local support providers and high-end users is deeper. The IT organization provides these deep target areas of IT support knowledge to establish the base for knowledge transfer.

The practical recommendations offered by the authors in this book provide campus leaders with a detailed agenda for action as they experiment with applications of knowledge management to the pressing needs of their colleges and universities. The thoughtful observations presented in these chapters should also stimulate strategic thinking about the role of knowledge management in higher education.

Index

by corporations, 4, 6; trends in, 12-16
Knowledge transfer, 108–110, 111
Koulopoulos, T. M., 3
KPMG Consulting, knowledge management spending by, 25–26

L

Latour, B., 54
Lave, J., 52
Learning, knowledge management linked with, 6
Legacy documents, Web storage of, 11
Leveraged support model of knowledge management, 99–110
Levitt, N., 36
Libraries, appropriation of knowledge management by, 30–32
Library and Information Service Commission (United Kingdom), 31
Lilly Endowment, 33
Lockard, T. W., 100
Lotus Notes, 12
Lyman, P., 35, 44, 47

M

Macintosh, A., 27
MacNeil, H., 86
Malone, M. S., 28
March, J. G., 83
Marx, G. T., 58
Massachusetts Institute of Technology (MIT), 27, 60
Massy, W. F., 47
McClure, P. A., 99, 100
McGee, J., xiii
McKemmish, S., 93, 94
McKinsey and Company, knowledge management spending by, 25
Moore, J. F., 38

N

National Science Foundation, 37, 50, 55
Netcentric information architecture, 70–71
Neural nets, 76
Ngin, P. M., 84

Nokia, 15
Nonaka, I., 58
Norris, D., 32

O

O'Dell, C., 9, 59, 68
Ohio University, 11
Olsen, J. P., 83
On-line analytical processing (OLAP), 74–75
Operational excellence, knowledge management applied for, 7, 10–11
Organizational records, 83–97, 119; archives of, 94–95; characteristics of, 84–86; creation of, 83–84, 86–87; evolving nature and scope of, 87–90; as knowledge assets, 90–94; rationales for managing, 92–94; strategic issues, 95–97

P

Patents, 28, 32, 57
Pattern matching, 27–28
Peebles, C. S., 35
Pennsylvania State University, 11
Polanyi, M., 3
Portals: corporate, 9–10; in higher education, 9–10, 13, 17, 18, 19, 20, 21, 22. See also Web sites
Porter, T. M., 112
Powell, W. W., 54
PricewaterhouseCoopers, 4, 6
Process engineering approach, 27–30, 116
Product launch, knowledge management applied to, 8
Productivity, as goal of information technology application, 47
Prusak, L., xiii, 28

R

Records. See Organizational records
Records Continuum Research Group, 86, 95
Rembrandts in the Attic (Rivette and Kline), 28

versity of Michigan), 53; Digital
Millennium Copyright Act
(DMCA) Agent, 62; to enhance
communication with students,
9–10; to improve operational excellence in higher education, 11;
Working Group on Digital Publishing in Archeology (UCLA), 53–54.
See also Portals

Webber, A. M., 28, 33
Wellman, B., 58
Wenger, E., 39, 52
Wilson, P., 8

Z

Zemsky, R., 47
Zuboff, S., 47, 58–59